2-20-88

D0834815

Kelly,

Letters To My Son

To Roxann

We substantiate our loved ones lives by the way we live ours. In doing so we create a legacy in their honor, and bring joy back into our hearts. We live in two spheres of existence, with love and the desire we can connect at that seam where our worlds meet. Love never Dies

Love + light
Mitch.

Letters To My Son

a journey through grief

by Mitchell D. Carmody

Beaver's Pond Press, Inc.
Edina, Minnesota

Note: *All pencil illustrations throughout the pages of this book are original works of art by the author. Signed limited edition prints of these and other works are available by contacting Heart Light Studios Inc. for more information.*

LETTERS TO MY SON © copyright 2002 by Mitch Carmody. All rights reserved. No part of this book may be reproduced in any form whatsoever, by photography or xerography or by any other means, by broadcast or transmission, by translation into any kind of language, nor by recording electronically or otherwise, without permission in writing from the publisher, except by a reviewer, who may quote brief passages in critical articles or reviews.

ISBN 1-931646-40-6

Library of Congress Catalog Number: 2002103123

Printed in the United States of America

First Printing: April 2002

06 05 04 03 02   6 5 4 3 2 1

Beaver's Pond Press, Inc.

5125 Danen's Drive
Edina, MN 55439-1465
(952) 829-8818
www.beaverspondpress.com

to order,
1-877-43(

Heartlight Studios

14765 70th St. South   Hastings, MN 55033
To order: www.heartlightstudios.net
Email: heartlightstudio@aol.com

Dedicated to my son, Kelly James Carmody, Travis and Jason [Carmody] Frost, David Carmody, Jimmy Carmody, Alexander [Carmody] Pope, Nettie Detviler, Sam and Sig Voje, Erika Hammond, Kody McGrath, Trevor Thielen, Bradley James DeGraw, Johnny Glass and to all the young children who left their loving parents too soon.

Neither can they die anymore: for they are equal unto the angels; and are the children of God.

—St. Luke 21:36

We do not need to proselytize either by our speech or by our writing.
We can only do so really with our lives…
Let our lives be open books for all to study.
—Mahatma Gandhi

Contents

Introduction

I believe one of the strongest challenges a person can experience in this life is the loss of a child. It is the single most traumatic and devastating reality that I personally have had to bear. There have been years of struggle, but I have found out that within that struggle miracles do happen; there is life after death on both sides of the equation. One can survive a significant loss and again find meaning in life and our lost loved one can help us do that. An important part in healing your grief is expressing your pain and your thoughts to them—that is a healing in and of itself.

Following the death of my nine-year-old son, Kelly James, on December 1, 1987, I wrote a series of letters to him as a panacea for my grief. He died following a two-year battle with a malignant brain tumor. Every few months I spontaneously penned him a letter when I felt the need to do so. There was no master plan or schedule that I adhered to; I just did it when I did it. For me it was a very valuable tool in processing my grief and letting go. I know that he received my letters, for he answered me back by fulfilling a request that I had made to him in one specific letter. That response was a miracle in and of itself and will be addressed later in this text.

The purpose of printing these letters and opening my soul and inner thoughts to others stems from a gift that my son has given me: to minister to others and help them to heal and ease the pain in the process of their bereavement. I found out that when you give, you truly do receive and in unexpected ways. Helping others has become of prime importance in my life and is a continuing healing for myself as well. It keeps his legacy alive when I see our lives touch the lives of others.

For it is in giving, that we receive.
—St. Frances of Assisi

May the pages of this book help to heal a part of your life or give you a tool to use in processing your own grief or helping others to process theirs. I believe that we can communicate with our loved ones who have passed on and they in many various ways can communicate back to us. If you are open to the universe many things can and will present themselves; all you need is faith.

To better understand the experiences, the magic and the miracles referenced in the letter/poems in this text one should know the history behind them. We were taken on a magical mystery ride that was and is life changing. That brief period in our lives has changed us forever. The prologue is an attempt to give you a consolidated version of our life prior to and following our son's death; I think it will provide the necessary framework to understand many details mentioned in the letters and poems.

—Mitchell D. Carmody

Prologue

*It may be the destination that is your goal,
but only on the journey—do you discover your soul.*
—Mitch Carmody

Bayport

We were the perfect American family residing in Bayport Minnesota in the early 1980's. In 1976, I married Barb Wohlers, my high school sweetheart. We soon became expecting parents and moved to this quaint little river town close to the Twin Cities. We bought a grand old gothic house built at the turn of the last century. We settled in comfortably and eventually had two children, a boy and a girl, Kelly and Meagan.

Besides having the typical dog and cat, we had a goat, rabbits, chickens, hamsters, fish, an iguana and other pets that came and went. I had built a huge deck with a wood fired sauna and hot tub attached. For the kids I had constructed a unique tree house that was built onto a hollow oak tree for which you had to climb into and up through the trunk to access the tree house.

Our house was located on a corner lot, just walking distance from Main Street and the St. Croix River. Summer was a very busy and happy time. Our yard was always filled with kids from the neighborhood. It seemed we could live there forever. We had good jobs; we were healthy, happy, and very content. Life didn't get much better than this.

Then things changed. On March 23rd of 1984, eleven days after my twin sister Sandy and I celebrated our 29th birthday together; she and her two boys were killed in a terrible auto accident. She left behind a very distraught husband, and a set of thirteen-month-old boy/girl twins. This event took the whole family by shock; it was a very difficult time for us all. Two years prior to this tragedy, my brother David had died after years of suffering with poor health due to severe retardation from an early age. I had lost my father to heart disease at age 15 and all my grandparents had died before I was age 25.

With all this death and tragedy in our family I thought I had a good grip on death and dying. I signed up for hospice volunteer training at a local hospital. They told me I had to wait one year following the death of a close family member. I patiently waited out the year and began my training late fall of 1985, completing it in February of 1986. It was then that our world fell apart.

On the last day of my hospice training, a small completion celebration was held. On the way home from that party, I met my wife's car on the road speeding madly in the opposite direction. I flagged her down and she pulled over. My son was resting on the seat next to her and all she said was, "Dear God Mitchell our son is very, very sick. We need to go to the emergency room NOW." Kelly was seeing double, throwing up and his head really hurt. At the hospital, x-rays confirmed the doctor's fears that Kelly had a brain stem tumor. The tumor was called a Medulloblastoma and it was as big as a baseball; it was malignant, fast growing, and deadly. It had to be removed immediately.

Our lives now concentrated fully on saving our son with any and all means at our disposal. Kelly went through three brain surgeries to treat and remove as much as possible of the malignant mass. We almost lost him twice through the process, and we were very frightened. When Kelly was able to speak again, he told us that he had seen the surgery. He began to recount that he had seen all the doctors and nurses around his body and cutting into his head. I questioned him about how did he see this and from where in the room? He said that he had "just kind'a left his body" and was up in the corner of the room holding hands with Jesus. Although I am very spiritual, I am not what you would call a bible thumper. I respect everyone's version of his/her godhead to be. I admire religious fervor and believe in miracles but my beliefs are not limited strictly to Christianity. Kelly was exposed to many different cultures. Whatever Kelly saw it was from no prompting from me.

I asked Kelly what Jesus looked like and he replied, "He looked like Half-Nelson—ya know, like one of my Garbage

4

Pail Kid cards." At that time these collectable gum cards were very popular with young boys because they were so gross. They were a rather grim card form parody of the then very popular Cabbage Patch Doll. Kelly adored these revolting cards and collected them voraciously; he had many. One of these cards was called: Half Nelson; it was a half boy and half girl depiction. Despite the ignoble nature of these cartoon caricatures, in the broader spiritual understanding, what Kelly describes makes perfect sense. The soul is androgynous, why not Jesus? The ultimate physical incarnation of the perfect spirit, which encompasses both the anima and animus. Take away our physical human cloak and there is only soul, be it man, woman, or child.

Three weeks later, Kelly returned home from the hospital very weak and was partially paralyzed on his right side. His prognosis was not good; he was given only 18 to 24 months of life expectancy *with* treatment. The treatment consisted of a strict regimen of chemotherapy and radiation as well as ongoing physical therapy. During this time he was often sick from the chemotherapy, but seemed to be growing stronger despite its' toxic effects. Our life was hospital visits as a daily routine and focusing on his recovery.

When Kelly was up to it, we traveled as much as possible; *"Carpe Diem,"* SEIZE THE DAY, became our motto! We took a quick train trip to Chicago one weekend to see the town and it's many museums. We traveled to Florida where we saw Disneyworld/Epcot as well as Disneyland and Universal studios in California where Kelly got to ride on E.T.'s bike.

In May, four months following his diagnosis and surgery, Kelly was back in school. It was a difficult challenge for him physically and emotionally. The surgery had left Kelly with serious right-sided weakness. He had a faltering gait and had difficulty writing with his right hand. Undaunted, Kelly learned to write with his left hand and was determined to be a

5

normal child in every way. He did well in school scholastically and soon overcame most of his physical challenges. Over the summer Kelly learned how to ride his bike again and even joined the T-ball team. There were ups and downs, bad and good days, but we seemed to be getting back into the mainstream of life. We were confident things would only get better.

To aid us on our journey, we had started a relationship with a very remarkable man by the name of Bernie Siegel. Bernie was a medical doctor, but not one of the many attending physicians in Kelly's case at Children's Hospital (or was he). Bernie was a surgeon in New Haven Connecticut who had written a book about fighting cancer. We saw a copy at Children's Hospital library, we read it, we liked it, and we embraced the philosophy it contained. The name of his book was *Love, Medicine and Miracles*.

Bernie was a well-respected surgeon who in 1978 had started a cancer patient support group called ECaP (Exceptional Cancer Patients). While studying the patients that he treated, he began to notice that the patients who took charge of their disease and were the biggest pain in the rear to deal with were the ones that went into remission more often. They fought to stay alive and questioned everything that was done to them. They wanted to know their disease and fight it with everything at their disposal. Many used holistic approaches that were physically non-threatening, easily done, and only complemented existing medical protocol.

This made so much sense; we took it to heart and began our own protocol to assist in our son's healing. We started to have Kelly draw some tumor fighting pictures—for instance, a drawing of *Pacman* eating way at his tumor. We also had him draw a goal picture for the future and one drawing of what ever he wanted to, just for fun. Eventually, we contacted Bernie in New Haven and began to send him Kelly's drawings so he could analyze them. Bernie would write us back and give us valuable feedback and support. We were so amazed and felt so fortunate that Bernie, a busy surgeon, author, lecturer and president of the American Holistic Medical Association would take time to send us handwritten letters and return our phone calls. This man was a remarkable physician for our son—as important as was his surgeon and the whole oncology team.

We did many things, but the most important part, beside our daily prayers, was our belief that what we were doing could make a difference. We explored the power of positive thinking, creative visualizations, guided imagery, the relaxation response, massage, placebos, crystal and light therapy, healing drawings, along with specialized diets using natural herbs and oils, and many other things. We wanted desperately to save our son; we explored numerous avenues that did not cause pain and could only help. It bolstered our energies and strengthened our focus. Bottom line—our son seemed to heal faster and experience less nasty side affects from the chemotherapy and radiation then he had before. He was feeling better physically, mentally and spiritually (we all were) than he had in months. Summer was in full swing and we actually started to feel like a normal family again. For the first time in months we started to believe that we could actually beat this thing.

Belief consists in accepting the affirmations of the soul; unbelief, in denying them.
—Ralph Waldo Emerson

In the fall, the kids started back to school and despite the difficult challenges Kelly entered the third grade with the rest of his classmates. We still had to take him out of school for his chemotherapy sessions, and it was at one of these sessions that Kelly told his mother about a questionnaire that he had to fill out at school. The children were asked to fill out a form answering questions about themselves, their likes, dislikes, favorite things, etc. One of the questions was: What makes you special? Kelly simply responded, "I'm alive." Together as a family we focused on this. We appreciated every day that was given us and our lives were full. Winter of 1987 crept in and we all hunkered down for the long cold season ahead, thinking only of positive thoughts for the spring.

Following a fairly comfortable long winter's nap, spring soon arrived and our lives were again propelled into pain and disbelief. In the end of May, just one year later from his initial return to school, Kelly went into a full-blown Grand Mal seizure on the playground and was rushed back into Children's Hospital. It was soon discovered that Kelly had a new fast growing, large tumor on the frontal lobe of his brain. My son was now given no hope for survival. Palliative radiation treatment was started to slow down the rapid growth of the tumor, but he was given only two months to live. We decided to split up his radiation schedule with two weeks on and then two weeks off. In between we planned a trip to Hawaii.

The Make-A-Wish organization granted Kelly a wish and at his request they agreed to send us to Hawaii for a week. The small, wonderful town of Bayport where we lived organized a benefit dance. With the help of our friends, Gina Polk's band *Zanth* and local Disc Jockey, Mike Wagner (a.k.a. Donuts), there was a tremendous turnout that raised over $12,000. This enabled us to go to Hawaii for two weeks instead of just one. We saved the rest of the money for the inevitable rainy days ahead.

Omnia Aliena Sunt, Tempis Tantum Nostrum Est.
Nothing is ours…except time.

Hawaii / Mexico

The trip to Hawaii was the highlight of our lives. The wonderful people there took us up in their arms and in their hearts. They treated us like royalty. They called Kelly their little brother and catered to his every need. Kelly said he must have lived here a long time ago because he felt like he had come home. His spirits started to soar in Hawaii away from the doom and gloom of home. The well-intentioned visits accompanied with casseroles, flowers, tears, and hugs had soon become a premature wake. We needed to get away as a family and recharge our spirits. We did not look back.

We left Hawaii feeling rejuvenated physically, and spiritually. Flying back we stopped in southern California to visit my nephew Jimmy who lived near San Diego. He was living with his estranged father, his father's wife and their three children. His father's wife, Francesca, was of Mexican descent; together they owned a little beach house in Mexico, on the western shore of the Baja Peninsula. In Minnesota we have cabins up in the north woods; in southern California it's beach houses on the Baja. The house was located in a small (non-tourist) fishing village just south of Ensenada.

In the village near their beach home, lived a woman who collected a wild herb called golendrina. With it she made a tea that had a purported healing affect that aided in the discomforts associated with cancer treatments. My nephew thought we should meet this lady. We had one day before we would fly home and begin more palliative radiation. We also needed to refill Kelly's anti-seizure medication. But for now it was Carpe Diem! We are off to Mexico.

Guided by my nephew's father, Butch, we drove down through Tijuana, past Ensenada to the peaceful sea village of

Maniadera. There we were introduced to Señora Doña Nieves, a gentile older woman well respected in the village. She offered us the tea that she had collected and would collect more if we needed it. She also mentioned that she had a vision of this blue eyed, blonde little boy from America that sought a healing from God. She said it was our son Kelly. She invited us to stay overnight and attend her chapel services in the morning. We had flight plans to leave the next morning but hey, Carpe Diem rules; flights can be changed; we stayed. Radiation can wait one more day.

We stayed the night at the beach house and the next morning began the most powerful life changing experience of our lives.

Doña Nieves (with instructions from God) had built a small chapel behind her modest home. It was to be used for healing and was decorated with pictures of those who had been healed in the past. We were instructed to wear light colored clothing and to bring fresh flowers for the altar. We were to only have love in our hearts while giving thanks to God for our expected healing.

Before we could enter the door of the chapel, Doña Nieves brushed our heads with fresh herbs and anointed us with strange pungent oil. We made the sign of the cross and were seated appropriately in the room in such a way that was to balance the energies. It all seemed so very ritualistic and strange. We hadn't a clue what was going to happen; all we knew is that it *felt* so right. Kelly also knew, for his face was illuminated with spiritual intrigue. Something powerful was working in this chapel, and we embraced it.

A few other locals and their family members arrived and were seated. The Doña lit incense and candles while continually splashing holy oil all around and on her body. She seemed to be in continuous prayer and beseachment. Soon two ladies arrived after having traveled a long distance by bus. They seemed to be important to the ceremony as they were greeted with much fervent prayer and hand waving. One of the ladies, Maria, an older almost toothless woman, was revered as a powerful spiritual healer and was seated in a hardback chair next to the altar. The other lady with her was Marta who seemed to assist Maria, and was seated on a bench located on a sidewall at the front of the church. Once everyone was seated, Doña Nieves began to speak and open the ceremony. Everything was spoken in Spanish, but fortunately my nephew's stepmother was bilingual and interpreted for us.

The service was a strange mixture of Mexican Catholicism coupled with local mysticism. Typical Catholic mass preliminaries were conducted and then the focus shifted to Maria. The little old woman had gone silent and seemed in deep meditation. She was rocking back and forth in her chair, breathing rhythmically in long, slow, inhales that whistled through the large gaps in the upper row of her teeth. In a trance like state, Maria slowly rose to her feet with arms outstretched and announced in a deep booming voice that our Lord Jesus Christ was here and speaking through this woman. We were asked, one at a time, to come up before our savior. Maria's persona now seemed to be gone, and Jesus was in the room speaking to us in the first person.

A strange very wonderful energy filled the air as she spoke. You could feel a tangible goodness, a powerful all encompassing energy shift taking place in the little chapel. It was as though we were being bathed in some incredible positive radiation that gave me goose bumps that would not recede. The palms of my hands were continually sweating, and a feeling of undeniable love filled my heart that brought tears to my eyes. Everyone in the room knew something very powerful and miraculous had just happened that was beyond our understanding. God had certainly gotten my attention.

Kelly was called up to stand before Maria. He was a little nervous, but feeling the magic that had entered the room, he nobly walked up to the altar unassisted. Through Maria, Christ placed His hands on Kelly's head while announcing that He was wrapping His purple robe of love around him and that the healing had now begun. He stated that He had placed three lights of healing into Kelly's heart that would be made evident to us within the week. Kelly walked back and whispered to me, "Wow, Dad, I really felt God's hands on my head."

Barb and I were each called individually, blessed, and given our gifts. I was told that I was to be an apostle of God and would be spreading the message of God's love. It was said that I had faith as big as a mountain and that I was to be the pillar of strength for my family and Kelly's healing. Barb was given the gifts of unconditional faith and was told she was to be an instrument of God's healing powers. Others were called up and given their gifts. Following the last person to receive their gifts, all were called up to stand in front of the altar. Maria then closed her eyes and dipped flowers into holy water and blessed us all. She then gave each one of us a bloom, with instructions to take them home and keep them next to our bed. Kelly was instructed to put his under his pillow for a week.

After this benediction, Maria sat back down and relaxed into her chair. In a few moments her whole body jolted into a severe spasm; she then slumped quietly into her chair and was very still. In a moment she seemed to regain her composure and you could tell that Maria was back.

Everyone was given a glass of holy water to drink, and the experience was discussed. There was now an excited and animated energy in the room and despite the language barrier you could tell something very wonderful and extraordinary had just taken place. Through interpretation we found out that the ladies were very confident that Kelly's healing would take place, but not without our help. We were told we needed to attend seven more Sunday services for the healing to become complete. They said the Lord would provide the means for our stay to be possible. Marta the other woman said that we all have lived previous lives before and that Kelly's life this time around was to bring people closer to God with the miracle of his healing. His healing would be known across the land, forever spreading the message of what faith in God can do. We were told to listen very closely to what Kelly had to say; the hand of God had now touched him.

The ladies closed the service with more hymns that were sung in their local Spanish dialect. Most of the locals joined in, as well as one other little voice: Kelly was singing right in tune with them IN PERFECT FLUENT SPANISH. Kelly did not know Spanish, much less a local dialect, and certainly did not know the ancient hymn. But sing he did! It was a miracle. *Gracias a Dios* (Thanks Be to God).

We were given some of the promised herb called golendrina that was to be used to make a healing tea as well as a poultice for Kelly's head. Doña Nieves collected this herb herself, high in the Sierra Mountains. Many years ago, an old Mexican shaman had shared with her the power of this herb and where to collect it. She said that it has helped many people in different ways. We were to make a tea and give it to Kelly three times a day orally as well as a poultice for his head three times a day. We were also asked to return to the chapel on Friday when some spiritual doctors would be arriving who would want to see Kelly.

We left the chapel that morning awe-struck, trembling, and crying tears of joy. The experience left us feeling highly exhilarated; yet drained at the same time. Something happened in there that was very real and quite powerful. We knew at that moment when Kelly sang in Spanish, God wanted us to stay in this little Mexican village. We also knew we had some very serious decisions to make immediately.

Kelly was still on anti-seizure medication, as well as Prednisone and was scheduled in a few days for more radiation back at Children's Hospital. This was a life and death decision to make for our son that could drastically affect the days and months left of his short life. The radiation schedule, which was palliative, would only slow down the rapid growth of the tumor, not cure him. We could hold off on this for a while and see what the next few weeks would bring.

Our biggest concern was taking Kelly off his seizure medication and the Prednisone. My wife who was in the medical field at the time was very concerned about the medical implications of taking him off his medication in this remote little village so far from a hospital. She decided it would be best to slowly taper what medications we had left until they were gone. The very best (and worst) of modern medicine had failed our son. There was nothing more the medical community could realistically offer him. We were very scared and uncertain but we put our faith in God and decided to stay at least until Friday so we could meet with the spiritual doctors. This would also afford us the time to discover what *three lights* of healing would be presented to us. We believed that the spirit of God had touched us, and He would continue to guide us on this new journey.

Let me assert my firm belief that the only thing
we have to fear is fear itself.

—Franklin Roosevelt

The Three Lights

My nephew's father said that we were welcome to stay at their beach house as long as we wanted to (*mi casa/su casa*: my house, your house). With that kind offer we unpacked our bags and went into the town of Ensenada to shop for supplies and find what God wanted us to find. We felt so connected and knew we would be guided to our three healing lights spoken of in the Sunday service. My wife's and my gut feelings were together on this and insights were becoming clearer and seemingly obvious.

While shopping for food, we came upon a natural health food store to which we were instinctively drawn. Once inside we discovered the store was also a holistic clinic owned and run by a medical doctor turned nutritionist/herbalist. He was also a certified macrobiotic consultant. Natcho, as we learned to call him, was an endearing man with a warm smile, penetrating blue eyes and who spoke excellent English. We soon found ourselves telling him the whole story of Kelly's illness from diagnosis, to the present moment. He was very excited about the possibility of being able to help Kelly with a macrobiotic diet. He prescribed a disciplined diet of whole grains, brown rice, seaweed, tofu products and herbs. There were to be no sweets or any sugars at all, no fruits, fruit juices or any dairy products. This was a macrobiotic healing diet to cleanse the body of the deadly residues and toxins from radiation, drugs, and chemotherapy. He also alleged that this diet could reduce existing tumor mass and mitigate further tumor growth.

We all decided to go on the diet and bought bags of macrobiotic vittles, spices and soybean product milk. Kelly was not too excited about the prospect of eating all this weird stuff (especially eating seaweed everyday), but it beat going back to the hospital and he accepted the idea very bravely. This was the first light of healing brought before us, just one day following the service.

I will have to admit I thought the food was disgusting and craved a nice juicy cheeseburger, but it was one for all and all for one. We did it together as a family, and we became quite resourceful with the limited allowable foodstuffs. The food had to be prepared in a specific way, and it soon just became part of our normal activities.

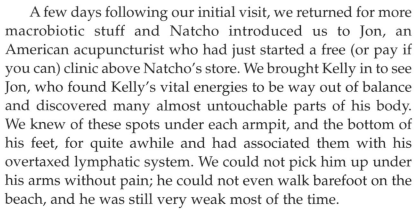

A few days following our initial visit, we returned for more macrobiotic stuff and Natcho introduced us to Jon, an American acupuncturist who had just started a free (or pay if you can) clinic above Natcho's store. We brought Kelly in to see Jon, who found Kelly's vital energies to be way out of balance and discovered many almost untouchable parts of his body. We knew of these spots under each armpit, and the bottom of his feet, for quite awhile and had associated them with his overtaxed lymphatic system. We could not pick him up under his arms without pain; he could not even walk barefoot on the beach, and he was still very weak most of the time.

Jon thought that together with Natcho's diet and visits twice a week for acupuncture that Kelly's vital energies could be restored, which would aid in his recovery. Jon said he had to consult with Sen Say, an old Japanese acupuncture master and mentor in San Diego. He did not feel qualified to prescribe the more precise treatments required for this difficult case. Until Jon could speak with Sen Say, he began initial treatments immediately on Kelly with the needles. Kelly relaxed and went with the flow saying: "Heck, dad, these needles ain't nothing. I can't feel a thing!" Thus we found our second light of healing as easy as the first.

For the next few days we relaxed on the beach, enjoying our newfound solitude and experimenting with our macrobiotic diet. On Friday we went again to the chapel to meet with the doctors that we were told would be coming. Doña Nieves greeted us and going through the same preliminary rituals we were seated this time in the back of the chapel. In the back there was positioned one single cot and a hardback chair, plus a single candle burning, as well as some incense. Fewer people were in attendance than there were on Sunday, but Doña Nieves, Maria, and Marta were still running the show. As Doña Nieves sprayed the pungent oil about and prayed, Maria seated herself in the hardback chair next to the cot. We were instructed to put our hands in our lap; palms upward, close our eyes, and pray.

Maria started her loud moaning and strange deep breathing that whistled eerily through her missing teeth. After a few moments, Maria stood up and in a different voice introduced herself as Emilio Pielroja from the tribe of David. *He* then proclaimed that he was a gifted surgeon that had come to operate on this child in the name of Jesus Christ. Wow...so this was the doctor we came to see! I thought we were going to see some in the flesh doctors with spirituality, not doctors *in the spirit*. This seemed very bizarre to say the least, but everything else had fallen into place thus far. We had to see it the rest of the way through.

This spirit doctor (through Maria) called Kelly up to stand in front of her. Maria then took a bunch of tied herbs and brushed them on Kelly's head and body. Praying all the while she then brushed the floor in a wide circle around Kelly, finally depositing the herbs into an old coffee can of holy water. Grabbing an egg from a bowl full of fresh eggs on the table, Maria made the sign of the cross with it on Kelly's forehead at the tumor site. She then placed this egg in the coffee can with the herbs. More eggs are removed and one at a time they are rubbed on the back of his head, the chest, and every joint of his body. These eggs were then deposited into the can of holy water as well.

The eggs, we are told, are supposed to pull out the sickness. Maria then stated she would have to perform surgery

17

to remove as much of the tumor as possible. I grab my wife's hand as we gasped together under our breath at this unusual admonition. Kelly seemed very relaxed and compliant with the situation. There was no evidence of scalpels or knives in Maria's hands so we relaxed (a little) and continued to observe and pray for strength.

Maria recited a prayer and then gave Kelly an injection of anesthetic (in pantomime, of course) into his arm. She then pretended to cut open the top and back of Kelly's head with some invisible tool. She methodically checked around the incision areas with her fingers, diagnosing the situation. With a look of acknowledgment on her face, she proclaimed that through the power of Christ this child shall be healed. She then grabbed Kelly's young head very compassionately with both gnarled old hands. Placing her ancient lips against his forehead, she began long slow sucking sounds. She increased her fervor and began sucking madly as if vacuuming out his entire brain. Turning Kelly slowly around, she then repeats this procedure on the back of his head.

Appearing somewhat shaken, Maria stepped back from Kelly for a few moments, regained her composure and asked for the coffee can of holy water with the eggs and herbs. She also requests for a glass of fresh holy water, which Doña Nieves provided for her. Maria takes a few small sips of the *fresh* holy water. After swishing it around in her mouth for a few moments, she spits out copious amounts of a white foamy yet slimy substance into the can. It reminded me of a melting marshmallow that slowly falls from a stick and into the campfire. She performed this spitting procedure several times, always accompanied with head shaking and a grimace of distaste stamped upon her face.

The can was then set on the vacant front pew. Pointing her finger at the can in dramatic gestures, she cautioned us strongly that the evil, the sickness, was in the can and that we should stay away from it, *"Que Muy Malo!"* (Very bad) she screamed. Within seconds there were flies swarming all over the can. It was disgusting! The Doña then reprised us once again, saying that the evil was attracting the flies and to stay away. The doctor then announced (through Maria) that we were to come back as many Fridays at it took until he (the doctor) felt the child had recovered fully from this surgery.

While Kelly was still with Maria (and the doctor), my wife, Barb, was called up to assist. Barb was given a small plastic medicine cup and was instructed to stand close to Kelly. Then Maria, chanting with her eyes still closed, pulled something from the air above her head. She then placed this invisible something into the cup in Barb's hand. Barb was told there were twelve pills placed into the cup, six white and six purple; the white ones were to be taken with water at 6a.m. every morning and the purple were to be taken each night at bedtime. Every time a pill was given, we were to say a prayer of thanks for God's healing and profess our love for God. The doctor also stated that he would come at 5 a.m. every morning while we were sleeping. At that time he would dress the wound and change the bandages as well as bless each and every one of us. Maria then sat down on the hardback chair, shook violently a few seconds, then after a slight pause, her small frame slumped quietly and was still.

In a few moments Maria stiffened, stood up and in a completely different voice and mannerisms, she spoke again. A Doctor Martíne had come through her this time. She (he) checked over Kelly quickly and rather brusquely. *He* then said to please follow any given instructions to the letter and everything would be fine; "Next patient please." She then proceeded to take care of the many ailments of the people in the chapel. When she was finally through with the last local seeking help, Maria fell back into her chair looking totally exhausted. Suddenly, she jerked violently and opened her eyes. Then standing up as if waking up from a long restful nap, she smiled and belched loudly in a very nonplused manner. Dousing herself with oil of balsam and acting like she had just arrived, she yawned and said she would see us on Sunday. We hugged her warmly and left feeling dazed and confused.

What the hell had we just gone through? I am a rational

man but I was clueless to what had just happened in there. You could sense, feel and hear the different personalities that emanated from Maria. It completely blew me away—my senses were reeling. Was this some bizarre cult? Were we being taken in somehow and not know it? Whatever it was, it did not matter. Bottom line...we all felt so loved. It felt so right and God help us, it felt so damn good to have hope again.

We were instructed to bring only flowers and our faith with us to the service, nothing more. We offered to pay the bus fare for the long ride Maria and Marta had to take, but we were refused. Nothing was asked of us except to keep our faith strong. Unconditional love costs nothing, and these people wanted nothing more than for us to allow them to do God's work and help heal his children. We had everything to gain. We rejoiced in our great fortune and walked home together hand in hand smiling real smiles for the first time in months. We had found the third light in these spiritual doctors and found that it was good.

Faith consists in believing when it is beyond the power
of reason to believe it.

—Voltaire

In the weeks that followed, we went to more Friday and Sunday services at the Doña's chapel. Many wonderful, strange, and miraculous things happened at those services and many were thankful. We received more spiritual medication and advice that we followed to the letter. My faith was strong, but some nights I would feel like an utter lunatic as I asked my child to pick up these invisible pills in an empty plastic cup. My faith always returned although, when Kelly would very casually pick the right color pill and would swallow it. Not only could he see the pills, he could feel them as he swallowed them. We continued with the acupuncture twice a week and maintained (as hard as it was) a strict macrobiotic diet. We slowly tapered Kelly off his *tangible* medications without incident, seizures, or problems.

In a strange quirk of coincidence, the acupuncturist placed the needles in the very same locations where Maria anointed Kelly with the sign of the cross on the Friday healing services. The acupuncturist also prescribed that we wrap a poultice of whole-wheat flour, taro root powder, fresh gingerroot and water around his head continuously. This was accomplished with a large bandanna that he wore on his head night and day. It was supposed to remove the heat of the tumor and reduce its size. When it dried out we changed it; it seemed to dry out very rapidly. In time we noticed that it required less frequent changing, as it was no longer drying out so fast.

Accompanying this change, we noticed Kelly was feeling better with a greater energy level. We could pick him up under his arms, and he would experience no pain. Kelly was out in the ocean on his boogie board and running on the beach *barefoot,* unheard of just a few short weeks ago. Something was definitely happening; our cautious optimism was turning into a real hope for the future. Hallelujah! It was a miracle.

On the sixth Sunday of our stay in Maniadera, we went to the little chapel with Kelly for the last time. We were told our son was healed, his tumor was gone and that we should go back to Minnesota to our material doctors and show to them what faith in God can do. They declared that our strong faith had healed our son and that his healing would be known all across the land. *Gracias a Dios.*

Nothing ever becomes real until it is experienced…even a proverb is no proverb to you until your life has illustrated it.
—John Keats

The Return

We returned to the United States and made plane reservations to fly home to Minnesota with a miracle in our pocket and hope in our hearts. Our major concern was Kelly's health and the continuation of methods of treatment that we had begun. God had given us a second chance; we wanted to maintain the status quo and promote further healing.

Before flying home and meeting with Kelly's doctors, we found a small house to rent in San Diego. We thought it best to stay in the San Diego area where Kelly's acupuncturist was located, to continue on with his protocol. We would still be near Mexico and be able to travel there for occasional church services to help sustain us in our faith. Our plan was to quickly return home to meet with Kelly's docs, and then return to California. We believed that his tumor was gone, but we needed to get the MRI done to substantiate the healing to the world.

The rental home we found was actually in Kensington, a quiet suburb of San Diego. We moved in immediately with only a few sticks of borrowed furniture. We still had a few days before our departure so we had the opportunity to accompany friends to a retreat area nearby in the Madre Grande Sanctuary Park. It was August 17, allegedly a very significant day in the cosmos where a once in a millennium planetary alignment was to take place. *"New Agers"* called this prophetic day the harmonic convergence, a day where simultaneously here and in places all around the globe people were gathering together to celebrate the birth of the Age of Aquarius. A new age, one hopefully filled with harmony and understanding, enlightenment, planetary healing and world peace. What better group of people, what better day, to celebrate the gift of our son's healing, our spiritual epiphany and our deep gratitude and love for God?

We participated in and experienced some wonderful things that day and evening. There were so many caring, loving people gathered in one place with so much shared belief in the power of love and healing. A large group of us participated in a rebirthing process that was very uplifting and energizing for us all. Afterwards, many people stayed behind to lay hands on Kelly and pray for his healing. Fully invigorated, we were now prepared to return home to face family, friends, and the medical community, with the news of our miracle.

Many people thought we had gone off the deep end or that we were somehow being taken advantage of. We were not crazy and we did not join some peculiar Mexican cult. We definitely had some incredible tales to tell, but crazy? No. The proof of Kelly's miracle was so obvious to us and it soon would be obvious to the world.

We returned home and immediately were brought down to the mundane realities of our house, our pets, unpaid bills, questioning neighbors and a very weedy yard. We looked at it all and let it go, for it had no power over us; we were participating in a miracle, and nothing else mattered. Breaking free of the confines of our experiential calluses and cautious optimism, we dared to believe that victory was ours. We believed that God had fulfilled his promise and healed our son. Now we had to get the material proof from our *material* doctors, that our hopes had come true and that we could confirm and substantiate the reality of our miracle. Our next stop was Children's Hospital— and the oncology team.

God heals, and the Doctor takes the Fee.
—Benjamin Franklin

At Children's Hospital we met with Kelly's primary oncologist to request that an MRI scan be performed. With a raised eyebrow he asked why we wanted this test done when we knew that there was no hope of a remission. We briefly explained the alternative methods of healing that we had experienced and that Kelly's condition had improved dramatically in so many ways. We wanted to know what exactly was happening. He said they would do the test, but cautioned us not to get our hopes up too much. The test was completed and the results were viewed and examined. It was revealed to us what we knew all along: *there was no sign of the grapefruit size tumor that was evident six weeks earlier!* All that was visible was a gray indentation in place of where the tumor had been. The side-by-side MRI scans that were taken months apart, spoke for themselves.

The oncologist suggested that possibly the early palliative radiation had done more than was thought possible. He also remarked that although he did not necessarily believe that our alternative methods of healing had produced these results, he did say: *"I guess we all have a lot to learn."* After the doctor left the room, the attending nurse jumped up and down with ecstatic joy, hugging and kissing us as we all thanked God together. Words fail to express fully the supreme joy and exaltation that we felt at that moment. We walked down the halls and out the door of that hospital hand in hand literally kicking our heels up for joy. Victory was ours. Praise God!

Driving home that day from the hospital, we were all giddy with emotion and riding high with the hope and joy that filled our hearts. Soon I noticed that Kelly was looking out the window at all the cars in the rush hour traffic with a very serious, almost sad look on his face. I said, "What's wrong son? Why the long face?"

"Dad, I don't understand why all those people aren't looking over here at us. Don't they know a miracle has just happened?"

To me every hour of the light and dark is a miracle.
Every cubic inch of space is a miracle.
—Walt Whitman

Dare to dream.

A Journey In Faith

Where do we go from here? That was the biggest question in our minds and hearts. We had been touched by the hand of God and experienced a miracle first hand. An experience such as this can change your life and that of countless many other lives forever. A miracle is analogous to the act of dropping a small stone into a calm pond. It sends out ripples in all directions touching hearts and changing lives *ad infinitum*. The miracle is a gift; it is faith, which activates that part of us, which receives internal divine guidance. Call it vivid dreams, visions, voices, a psychic connection, spirit guides, or guardian angels—it all boils down to relying on that good old "gut feeling."

We had gone this far relying on our gut feelings and had made some extremely important life-changing decisions very quickly. We had dropped off the edge of the earth for six weeks and now had come back with a miracle. Some friends and family thought we may need deprogramming or that we were being ripped off in some way. Others had no idea what had happened to us. We had a lot of phone calls to make.

Word spread rapidly of our return and the miracle of Kelly's healing. It hit the local newspapers and radio waves. Soon we were inundated with calls. We relayed the story with great enthusiasm and spiritual fervor. It was like we were plugged into some powerful God energy that could not be dissipated. Nothing was an obstacle, any problem too large or people too small. Nothing could stop the momentum of our miracle in action. We had to continue with the plan that God had prepared before us. Kelly's tumor was gone, but our journey had only just begun.

Barb and I arranged for a further leave of absence from our employers, which was readily granted. Barb and Kelly flew back to the little rented bungalow in San Diego to continue on with Kelly's treatments. Little Meagan and I stayed behind in Minnesota for two more weeks. In those two weeks, I put the house on the market, sold most of what we owned, and arranged for placement of pets and plants. I rented a 14-foot U-Haul truck and packed it up with the bare necessities of life. I hitched up my wife's car to the back of the truck, and we said our good-byes. Meg and I were off to join our family in San Diego.

In San Diego we put the kids in school, found jobs, and prepared to make a new life. It was not easy but we made it work and continued with Kelly's alternative treatments. This new period of relatively calm times was short lived however, for within a month Kelly was getting sick again. At the hospital, it was confirmed that the cancer was back and that it was spreading rapidly throughout the brain and down the spine. It was *post-haste* back to Minnesota to be with friends and family. Kelly was dying.

The dark clouds were back. It felt as if though we had been kicked in the gut. We had so much hope and had worked so hard. We had done everything humanly possible to save our son—there was nothing more that we could do. It was so unfair. We were angry at God, angry at ourselves, angry at the acupuncturist, angry with the little Mexican church, angry with the doctors who could do no more and just damn angry at the world. It is probably this anger that gave us the needed energy to move halfway across the country one more time. Kelly and Meagan needed us more than ever and we needed to be home.

Barb made arrangements to fly back to Minnesota with both kids and stay with her mom and dad. I stayed in San Diego to pack up, settle affairs and await the moving van that my wonderful mother-in-law had graciously arranged and paid for. Once back home we rented a townhouse by the month; a place to set up hospice care and a place for Kelly to die. We traveled a little and celebrated Kelly's ninth birthday with all his friends and family. We had an emotionally difficult Thanksgiving, as it is hard to be thankful when your child is dying. We were preparing for that fact. No more efforts were made for a cure, just comfort measures and to allow Kelly to live his life to the fullest that his abilities would allow.

By the end of November, Kelly was very weak and sleeping later in the mornings. A Minnesota winter was now in full swing with its snow, ice, and cold north winds. December was just around the corner, and I was afraid Kelly would not see another Christmas. Most of our days were consumed with short walks, hot baths, and watching movies. On the last Sunday in November after a typical leisurely morning, we took the kids to see the movie, *Planes, Trains, and Automobiles*. John Candy was one of Kelly's favorite actors, and he was anxious to see the movie. We were all laughing very hard during the film, (a very welcome catharsis) but we soon noticed Kelly was getting quiet and fidgety; he wanted to go home.

We left the theater, stopped by a video store and picked up some movies. We gave Kelly some of his liquid morphine (which we had been using with greater frequency), gave him a hot bath, and set him up on the couch to watch some movies. The tumors in the spine made it difficult for Kelly to sit in a chair for a long period of time. Lying on the couch with lots of pillows and blankets was where he seemed most content and relaxed. In a few hours Kelly announced that he just wanted to go to bed for the night. It was only 4:30 in the afternoon but Kelly knew what he needed, so together we crawled into my bed for a late afternoon nap.

Curled up in our warm waterbed with daylight fading into darkness, I started to drift off to sleep staring at my son's beautiful face. Kelly seemingly aware of my gaze, slowly opened his eyes, reached over and very weakly brushed the back of his hand against my stubble of a beard and said, " Dad…I love you." With that said he rolled over and went immediately to sleep. I told him I loved him as well, tucked in his covers, and kissed him on the head goodnight. Now realizing that there were tears pouring down my face, I got up out of bed; something was happening. Kelly knew it, and I felt it.

At 7:30 in the evening Kelly came stumbling out of our bedroom looking dazed and confused. He said, "What happened? Where's mom?" I told him that after we had gone to bed for our little nap, Mom had gone shopping. Kelly replied that he had not remembered coming home from the movie or even going to bed, and he was confused that it was so dark outside. Clearly perplexed, Kelly looked at me very seriously and said in an exasperated tone, "Dad I need to clear my head, let's go for a frigging walk!" I hugged him tightly and said, "Sure son, I need to clear my head too." We dressed warmly and went for a short walk. Kelly was tired most of the time now, was becoming incontinent, and he was requiring stronger doses of morphine more consistently. I knew that his last days were approaching quickly and as far as I was concerned, he could do or *say* anything he wanted to.

The next day we called our neighbor Bonnie, a friend and certified hospice nurse to come and see Kelly. We told her of his recent changes and that we would appreciate her opinion on his condition. We were now preparing for his death; it was becoming real and we needed assurance that it was. Bonnie spent several hours with us and observed Kelly very closely. She told us that Kelly was indeed exhibiting classic symptoms that precede an imminent death. She felt that Kelly had only days left, possibly a week or two, but it was evident he was slowly slipping away. He could easily slip into a coma or die at anytime. We had no plans for dramatic life saving measures—only pain relief, comfort and lots of love.

After Bonnie left, I went shopping for a three-week supply of groceries, and other necessary comfort items that we may need. Kelly slept for most of the day. My wife Barb made all the necessary phone calls to family and friends to inform them that indeed Kelly was dying. "Come visit very soon," she said.

Later that evening two of Kelly's best friends, Jason and Dustin came over to say good-bye to Kelly. Kelly was very weak and was unable to communicate with them, but he was fully aware of their presence. Although he did not talk with the boys, he did raise his hand slightly and weakly waved good-bye as they departed. His left eye was now staying open all the time and needed constant wiping and lubricating. Kelly was no longer interested in food and even drinking water had become difficult. We only moved Kelly from couch to bed or to the bathtub as needed. As weak as he was he did not want to be carried, and we would walk him like a marionette. Evening soon turned to night and we *all* slept with one eye open, unsure what tomorrow would bring.

The next day was December 1, and Kelly for the most part was unresponsive on the couch; his lips and nails were turning blue and he was still and very pale. Bonnie (the hospice nurse) came over, as well as many close friends and family, knowing this would probably be his last day with us. We sent our daughter off with the Scheels, good friends from Bayport who took her out for pizza and an escape from the death vigil. They would call us with a number where they could be reached, should his condition worsen.

Our daughter Meagan was only five years old and needed a break, but she did not want to be gone too long from her "brover" and we wanted her there should Kelly pass on. While Meagan was gone Kelly's breathing became very erratic and shallow, Bonnie said, "Its time. You better get a hold of Meagan quickly."

The Scheels had called previously with a number at the pizza place where they had gone and we frantically called it, talked to them, and said, "Please hurry." Kelly's breathing was now very shallow and the death rattle evident. Time was of the essence; we were not certain Meagan would make it home in time. Kelly had now been totally unresponsive for hours, and with his breathing rate we knew it would only be minutes. Barb and I were kneeling next to Kelly, holding his hands, praying Meg would be there soon. Suddenly we heard a knock at the door, followed by Meg's cheery voice, "I'm home, Kelly."

At that moment Kelly opened his eyes, moving them toward the sound from the door. When Meagan reached the three of us on the couch she grabbed Kelly's hand and said, "bye bye Kelly, I love you. Sorry I'm late."

He looked at her and sighed one last breath. You could feel

that his spirit was leaving his body. His whole face previously paralyzed on one side, now relaxed. His eyelids opened slowly, revealing those beautiful cornflower blue eyes that glowed bright and clear with a look of serenity and peace. I could even see a twinkle in those eyes, as if he had just discovered some great secret. When his face relaxed, Kelly's smile also returned. It was a smile we had not seen in almost two years. Looking out at no one (that *we* could see), the light in his eyes faded and his lids slowly closed. The spark gone—forever.

Now that Kelly had died, we had to make arrangements for the body, as well as calling the local sheriff to report his death. We also made many phone calls to friends and family that were not present at the time of his death. With Kelly still lying on the couch in the same position that he had died, many friends and family showed up to give their last respects and support us in our time of need. In that tiny townhouse together with close friends and family, we laughed, we cried, looked at photo albums and shared many stories well into the evening.

When our minister, the reverend Mary Marcoux, arrived she was surprised to see that Kelly's body was still lying on the couch. We had many candles lit and were playing Christmas music as she walked in. She later commented it seemed more like a Christmas party then the scene of a recent death. She said it was awe-inspiring; a celebration of life that brought tears of joy to her eyes and not those of pain. There were angels in the room with us that night and who so ever entered that room *felt* it.

It was not until much later that the sheriff and the coroner showed up to witness the death and remove the body. I picked up my son's body to carry him down to the awaiting hearse when my brother-in-law Paul stopped me before I descended the stairs. He said, "Mitch, as Kelly's godfather, I held him as he was baptized, can I please hold him once more?" There at the top of the stairs I passed my son over to Paul once again, as I had done nine years earlier—only this time he kissed him good-bye.

We had already begun funeral plans while Kelly was alive. We made it a celebration of life and the miracle that was Kelly. The church was filled with hundreds of people many of whom were children. Numerous endearing stories were shared and joyful songs were sung. We had no graveside interment; Kelly's ashes were sent to Hawaii where friends released them from an airplane into the live volcano Mauna Loa. In lieu of a stone marker, we purchased a wall plaque at Children's Hospital with his signature and the words, *"Let your heart-light shine."*

Kelly experienced a healing in Mexico but, unfortunately, it was not a cure. I learned through the whole experience that there is a big difference between a healing and a cure. Sometimes they may happen together but usually I believe they are separate things—one spiritual, the other physical. We experienced both, but it was the spiritual healing that has endured and enriched our lives, and has hopefully made this world a little better place.

The physical aspect of healing, (i.e. a cure), is at its best intrinsically limited, for life by nature is terminal. We accept both the physical death and the spiritual healing. The first to be able to move on with our lives and the latter to more fully embrace our own spirituality. We must grow from our experiences to help nurture ourselves, our family and help to heal the human condition in general. Look for the gift encapsulated in your grief and find the golden opportunity that is presented to you. Share your life and you will find that through helping others in their pain you will alleviate yours, for it is when you give that you truly do receive.

You must give some time to your fellow men. Even if it's a little thing,
do something for others—something for which you get no pay
but the privilege of doing it.
—Albert Schweitzer

FROM KELLY—
TO MOM, DAD AND MEG

song lyrics by Laurie Pelnar

I didn't mean to make you cry
But you know I had to say good-bye
I loved you so and I know you know
I'll stay real close beside you
I'll be the light, the light that guides you

Look for the star the brightest one
That one that shines beyond the sun
I'll shine for you and see you through
With loving warmth and laughter

The tears will pass into a song
A song to echo your whole lifelong
Know I love you and I'll always be
The light that guides your fantasies

When you think of me please let it be
With rainbows and with laughter
The hurt will pass the love will last
Look for light, the light that guides you

You gave me everything I could have wished
Your smiles your laughter and your kiss
You made my life a fantasy; my last days were ecstasy
now I'll be the light, the light that guides you.

You are the light of the world. A city set on a hill cannot be hidden. Men do not light a lamp and put it under a bushel basket. They set it on a stand where it gives light to all in the house. In the same way, your light must shine before men so that they may see goodness in your acts and give praise to your heavenly Father.

—Matthew, 5:14–16

Suffering will come, trouble will come—that's a part of life
—a sign that you are alive.

—Mother Theresa (May 1975)

The Letters to Kelly

The seven letters I had written to Kelly are printed here in their entirety as they were written and have not been edited. I did not want to lose any of the emotion that was present at the time of the writing. Following each of the letters is a brief postscript from today's perspective. Not only is this a reflection of that period of time when the letters were written but also it provides details that support statements or settings mentioned in the discourses with my son.

Following each postscript are several poems that I had written at or around the time that each of the letters were written. The poems were written for others who were experiencing grief in their lives or simply for the solace of my own soul. Regardless of their inspiration, they vividly portray the emotions that I was feeling at that time. They also tend to illustrate the stage or combination of stages of the many elements of grief: Shock, Denial, Anger, Hope, Isolation, Bargaining, Depression and Acceptance. They are stages that you can and will experience as you process your loss. No one grieves the same way or on the same schedule. It is a rollercoaster of emotions that come as they may. You grieve as *you* grieve, and it takes as long as it takes.

To every thing there is a season, and a time to every purpose
under the heaven: A time to be born, and a time to die.
—Ecclesiastes iii-1

FOR A DYING CHILD

If fish could only half swim
or birds half fly
like an agreement to be half in love,
then maybe a child could half die—
with an agreement to be back in time.
How much easier the parting could be
knowing the promise of return.

But fish swim full hilt
and birds hit the air without remorse
most lovers would jump over the moon
to be overheels in love.
So a child dies and all we can do
is believe in his soul.

If we believe in this
and the new life that is his,
we may have more in common
with him
than with the living.

—by Nancy Lee Carmody (Kelly's aunt)

First Letter
February 20th, 1988

Why am I so special?
—I'm special because I'M ALIVE.

—Kelly Carmody (1987)

February 20th, 1988

Dear Kelly,

    It has been almost three months since you have left us and I miss you terribly at times. I replay your last few days over and over. I feel that I should or could have done more. I knew your time was very close, but then again I didn't really know how close. It was hard to see you degenerate so quickly, feeling impotent to change the devastating progression moving through your body. You were barely speaking and I sometimes wondered if you knew what was going on. I know you did not want to talk about death and I understand why. You wanted to live each moment without the realization of the shadow of death that was so obviously imminent. When you did make your transition, you looked so happy and at peace.

    It took a lot of guts and strength with pure love to wait for your sister Meagan to come home before you left. You really did love her a lot, didn't you? I know she misses you a lot, although she is enjoying the attention she gets now that you are not the center of our universe.

    Your funeral, as I am sure you saw, was breathtaking! It touched all that were present and will for years to come. You gathered quite a faithful following, my son, and have changed many lives in your short term here. You must be resting for quite awhile after such a long arduous battle. I am looking forward to a visit from you sooooooo much! I don't want to try too hard, but I am always ready when you are up to it ol buddy.

    I remember our short little walks around the snow and ice of that awful townhouse. Those walks were precious to me son, and it does hurt to think about it. I remember with joy our trip to North Carolina. I know now it was something you had to do before you left. I am so glad we did it and you did so well out there.

We had a kind of non-existent Christmas without you there, pal. It seems like I slept through it with vague dream memories. I am sure your Christmas was much better, probably more of a birthday party. Which reminds me how glad I was to have had your birthday party; I still watch the videos of it and ache.

I loved your message of your signature left in the pew at church and the "I'm Alive" song on the radio after the funeral you arranged for us to hear. Very subtle! Now get back with the code word to somebody, you turkey.

I hope you were happy with the shadow box I made for Mom from you. I felt guided by you to do it. It was symbolizing your moment of separation from the body as your spirit flew up the rainbow to unite with God. I wanted to keep your healing stone in a safe place, so I placed it inside. Your Mom is doing much better; you must be helping her now that you have rested a bit. Visit her soon son and wrap your arms around her and let her gaze into your beautiful blue eyes; then get to Meg and finally to me, Bubba.

How do you like our new house? Isn't it beautiful with the pond and everything? You would have loved it here, I know. We are doing the best we can to rebuild our lives without you and try to find happiness and joy again. I love your mother and sister very much and will do anything to make them happy. I think this new house is a good idea and we shall heal faster with it.

I am glad that you can now play with your dog, Maple again, as he has joined you recently. Have you seen Grandpa and Grandma Carmody, as well as Grandpa and Grandma Great? I bet you have seen Aunt Sandy with Jason and Travis already. I am feeling pretty good now Kelly and it is no reflection on my love for you. I just know you are where it really is at and we have to come home to you. But until that day, please pay us a visit. I MISS YOU SO MUCH!

If you can arrange for a sign from you this spring, like something growing from our yard, that would be neat and I WILL notice. I will write again later sometime. Know that I love you and still need your love.

—Dad

This was the first posthumous letter I had written to my son. It was penned some three months following his death. It reflects the post-shock period that soon follows the wake/ funeral and the subsequent intense grieving period. During the eighteen months that we battled with his cancer from its onset to his death, we had totally focused our lives on his recovery. Now our lives were focused on accepting his loss and working on our own recovery.

The funeral service at the church was packed with people, with many children sitting in front of the altar. In the back there was standing room only. We had the church filled with purple helium balloons that were then taken outside the church following the service and released into the cold December sky. Across the country friends and relatives released balloons at the same time. As we were leaving the church my niece came running over to me and said, "Look what I found." She had been rummaging through the envelopes on the backrest of the pew and found one that had been written on. It was Kelly's signature! The last time he had been in that church was seven months earlier.

When we had lived at the Mexican beach house, Kelly discovered an old Neil Diamond album. Kelly at the time was into heavy metal and rap music but seemed drawn to this album. On the album there was one song that Kelly really liked called *"Ensenada,"* which was where we were staying. The album also had a song that Kelly loved and played over and over again, it was called: "I'm Alive." The verses were so appropriate and reflected Kelly's positive attitude in Mexico. I had never heard of this song before and have only heard it on the radio once since those days in Mexico.

After the funeral was over and we went to some close friends' house for refreshments—I heard it again. We had been at the house several hours, and I went out to warm up the car (December in Minnesota) and once it was running, the radio started playing *I'm Alive,* right at the beginning of the song. I ran quickly inside and got my wife and friends; together we listened to that song in the cold winter evening and cried. Tears of pain, mixed with tears of joy, for we knew Kelly was saying that he was TRULY alive. This was the beginning of some very important spiritual affirmations that lifted our hearts for those first few months following his death.

Following this intense period of eighteen months, there was a tremendous feeling of relief. Together with the love and energy from family and friends, we felt buoyed up despite our pain. We bought a new house—nice suburban rambler on the edge of a park. My wife and I returned to our old jobs, our daughter Meagan returned to school and made new friends. After three months, the cards had stopped and most people thought we were getting on with our lives and things were getting better. Very few people know the true depth of your pain and how long it can last.

What shall we do with this strange summer, meant for you—
Dear, if we see the winter through
What shall be done with spring?
—Charlotte Mew

HELLO AND NOT GOOD-BYE

My son you have seen the worst of times
but yet have seen the best
life may have seemed unfair to you
up to this your final rest.

We did everything that we could do
to remove the evil curse
the disease that caused such misery
and eventually got worse.

This evil thing has taken your life
and violated your chance to live
cut short your youth's vitality
with all it had to give.

It may seem hard to understand
that good can come from bad
that happiness and joy can come
from times so very sad.

But good things have already happened
as now you can clearly see
your vision of a higher power
that sets our spirit free.

You have given the Lord to us
in ways no one ever could
made our eyes to see his light
our hearts to feel his good.

We have seen his miracles
made possible through you
although your life was very short
you brought us hope…that grew.

A stronger faith in our Lord
a deeper love in our hearts
a different way of looking at life
in all its intricate parts.

So my son, your life was not wasted
but shared with all mankind
and everyone, if we look
will find the tie that binds.

The tie that binds all human hearts
to each and one another
and when death does come our way
its shared by each sister and brother.

So today we are sharing you
a celebration of your life so brief
the saying of our unsaid good-byes
and the beginning of our grief.

Grieve we must for our tragic loss
for your eyes so heavenly blue
sorrow for the empty void
that was once filled by you.

Our grieving will not be easy
in fact it will be long endured
we all loved you so very much
and had hoped you would be cured.

But you have ascended to the Father
a fact we must accept
and for all you have given us
we are forever in your debt.

Good-bye my son, you're in good hands
though I will miss you in my own
but I will see you always
from the seeds that you have sown.

Thanks for having been my son
I'm proud to be your dad
and until our souls again unite
I'll remember all we had.

Now as you soar on eagle's wings
over rainbows in the sky
whisper to me upon the breeze
hello and not good-bye.

It is never any good dwelling on goodbyes.
It is not the being together that it prolongs,
—it is the parting.

—Elizabeth Asquith Bibesco

FEBRUARY 14TH, 1988

for Barbara

My darling I am not sure what to say
nor even what to do
to make this very special day
unique and true to you.

We have gone through so many things
from last year at this time
traveled our country over
from frigid to tropical clime.

Experiencing great joy and loss
alternating and together
clinging desperately to our faith
bound to a cancerous tether.

No one can truly be ready
to do what we had to do
be prepared to battle
and yet to each other remain so true.

True to our own identity
and true to us as a whole
putting all our strength together
to fight a common goal.

Cancer had declared war on us
we dared to fight back
examining life's priorities
and picking up the slack.

A battle plan was made
our enemy defined
we geared up with ammunition
a declaration of war was signed.

Sacrifices had to be made
we were motivated to win
no obstacles were ever too large
no ice ever to thin.

We forged weapons of pure energy
that were smelted in our hearts
with guidance from our God
and the knowledge that He imparts.

He informed us where to go
told us what to do
with us every step of the way
in places old and new.

We had many victories
but also suffered loss
their outcomes as flippant
as a coin in mid-air toss.

Though many battles were won
we lost the two-year war
as cancer beat the victim
and claimed the final score.

The scars of war are very deep
and takes time to heal
as any survivor of any war
can tell you how we feel.

Everything has to be rebuilt
future plans made anew
many things to overcome
before our healing is through.

Post-war years can be very hard
with flashbacks of hurt and pain
the causalities find a better life
it's hard work for those who remain.

But hard work we are used to
as together we can fight
the hassles of the present
to make the future bright.

We have always had each other
though differences there may be
communications can break down
setting trouble free.

I know that we can handle it
our love is very strong
our souls are bonded together
to last a lifetime long.

That lifetime is here and now
I have never loved you more
and someday as a family
on eagle's wings we'll soar.

Until that glorious day
when we reunite with our son
we'll live each day the best we can
praising God when the day is done.

A little while, and ye shall not see me: and again, a little while,
and ye shall see me, because I go to the Father.
—St. John, 16:16

Second Letter
April 2nd, 1988

And when life's sweet fable ends,
Soul and body part like friends;
No quarrels, murmurs, no delay;
A kiss, a sigh, and so away.
—Richard Cradshaw
'Temperance' (1652)

April 2nd, 1988

Dear Kelly,

What can I say except that I miss you terribly!!! The past week my thoughts have been on you every minute of the day it seems. I watch TV and see ads for a new horror film and I think of you, I see ads for a new monster toy and I think of you. We went on a hayride last week and I thought of how much you would have enjoyed that.

Tomorrow is Easter Sunday and we are reminded of the resurrection of our Lord. It is hard for me to feel anything except sadness. I see other fathers with their sons and it cuts through me like a knife. I know eventually things will hurt less and I know you are in the best of all places, but I cannot help feeling lost and helpless.

It seems I am covered by a thin invisible film of despair that cannot be shed or penetrated from within or from with-

out. I do not know if this film will last a lifetime and I will learn to live with it or it will eventually dissipate. I love our new home, your mother and Meagan dearly, but the desire to be with you is very strong. I would never dream of exiting this life on my own accord, but I could easily leave without remorse. These are my feelings now and it does not take away my love and devotion for your mother and sister. The reality is we are and will be here until our missions are through. I know I will find joy again but never quite the same intensity of joy.

I still am longing for a visit from you and I will do more on my part to try and communicate. Please find the strength to come to me. Sometimes I feel we kind of pushed you out the door, wanting the "unknowingness" to be over with. I admit in certain ways I did want it to be over, not knowing what else to do, but more than that was seeing you waste away to a shell like my brother David was something I could not bear to see. I hope you have had a long rest and will help me find my way! Be with me at the Indian sweat lodge next Friday if it can be arranged.

I love you forever.........Dad

This letter to Kelly was written five months following his death and illustrates the end of the "up" period that the first letter reflected. Nobody, except for some very special friends, ever brought up Kelly's name and we were expected to slide right back into the groove of normal life. The relief we now felt turned into a cavernous void that seemed impossible to fill. We had done so much for so long that initially the void was a period of physical, mental, and emotional rest that gave us the illusion of doing okay. Soon the void turned from rest to restless. We were used to doing so much and being so focused that we now felt lost and without purpose. I started feeling guilty for not having done more and especially guilty for the nights that I would check on him, praying that God would take him, to end the madness and the pain.

The Godsend that helped out during this time was the Indian sweat lodge that I referenced to in the second letter. I had heard of the Native American sweats held on Prairie Island and that the tribal chief at that time was Amos Owen, who had a vision to bring the healing power of the sweat lodge to non-Indians. I definitely needed a healing but, more importantly, I was worried about my wife. She was not doing well at all. I could attend the sweat ceremony, but she could not because she was in her phase of the moon (menses), which is not allowed. I fasted for a three-day period and then went to the sweat lodge alone. This particular evening there were a lot of people in attendance, which required that they hold two ceremonies in order to accommodate everyone who had traveled there.

Being a new initiate, I had to wait for the 2nd ceremony, which did not start until after 10 p.m. My wife had expected me back by that time, so, tired of waiting up for me, she had gone to bed. When I was in the sweat lodge, time lost all meaning, with the drums, the chanting, and the intense heat it became a different world. Amos said that this special ceremony was for the healing of all the relations and we passed the pipe of burning sage and beseeched the ancient grandfathers to come to the lodge and take our healing requests. An incredible feeling of peace and power filled the small enclosure. Healing requests were made and tears were shed freely that commingled easily with the rivers of pervasive sweat. I requested that the grandfathers go to my wife and give her a healing, one that she so desperately needed. When the sweat lodge ceremony was over, I sat by the fire awhile lost in the reverie of one of the most powerful spiritual experiences of my life.

I arrived home well after midnight and I was surprised to find my wife still up. Her face was radiant and she was smiling and crying at the same time. "Tell me about your sweat ceremony, Honey, but first let me tell you of the most incredible experience I had tonight." She said she had retired early at about 10 PM figuring the sweat was running behind. Later on, she awoke with a start at about 11 PM to hearing Kelly calling her name. She got up and walked out on to the upper patio deck and there she felt the presence of Kelly surround her. He said that he loved her and was happy and she could feel him hugging her and could actually smell his wonderful smell. Barbara looked so beautifully radiant and happy as she relayed this, that I knew it to be true. She had this experience at the same time as I had beseeched the grandfathers to go to her aid.

In this letter I had asked Kelly to be at the sweat lodge with me. I know with the help of the grandfathers that he was there and they had guided him to his mother when she needed him most. God works in mysterious ways as we have been finding out. There are miracles out there just for the asking. All you need is faith.

These incidents helped immeasurably in the healing process but it still takes a long time. There is no way around grief, only through it and it takes as long as it takes. The poem *Empty Fullness* that immediately follows this postscript was written the day after I wrote the 2nd letter to Kelly and truly depicts what my feelings were at the time.

Ah! little at best can all our hopes avail us
To lift this sorrow, or cheer us, when in the dark,
Unwilling, alone we embark,
And the things we have seen and have known
and have heard of, fail us.

—Robert Bridges
On a dead child, Stanza 7

EMPTY FULLNESS

What is this grip that holds captive my soul;
clenching my heart so hard to console?
Where is life going, what does it mean?
The mystery of life is yet to be seen.

Did I not have lofty ideals and dreams?
Carefully plotted plans die also it seems.
The future seems non-existent; each hour is now;
the past, a flood of pain, that I endorse and allow.

The pain is reality and breaks the omnipresent spell
with it comes a clarity…a crack in the shell
It lets the real world in for only a moment or two
and in that instant, I know I'll get through.

The pain rings clear of the awful truth of perdition
not a statistic or concept but the reality of condition
A glimpse in the darkness that the loss is for real
and gut-wrenching agony is all that I feel.

The aching diminishes as non-reality returns,
everyday life carries on, while my sorrow still burns.
I have traveled this path many times before
and recognize the signs that can open the door.

I cannot seem to find the panacea for my grief,
what had worked before, now gives no relief.
I seem destined to be caught in this web of non-being,
that feeling of empty fullness…perception without seeing

This space in time seems not to progress,
everyday seems like a dream that was dreamt in duress.
This feeling of futility I hope will transcend;
I have so much to learn and more to comprehend.

There is so much I want to do and my love I want to share,
I need again to smell the flowers and heal my dark despair.
Someday the light will come and illuminate my way
shadows will fade and so will the gray.

The sun will rise with beauty; I will again feel its embrace;
the rain will feel good once more as it falls upon my face.
The wind will blow sweet fragrances that I can smell anew
rainbows will again be enchanting in all their glorious hue.

Tomorrow will again have meaning; the past won't hurt so much.
God will walk by my side and again I will feel his touch.
Life plans can once again be made, dreams once more fulfilled,
daily living can carry on, the spirit no longer killed.

Life experiences will again have depth, feeling good will be the norm.
Energy consumed by our lament will take a different form.
Hope and joy will come again to fill our home once more
and songs of happiness and songs of love will issue from our door.

MY SOUL'S ON FIRE

God help me, my soul is on fire.
My heart labors beneath my breast.
I cannot understand what is going on,
is this some awful test?

What justice is there
when a child has to die;
the world is full of terrible people
why Lord, why my child, why?

The pain is so severe
I can think of none that is worse.
What has brought me to this day
what has sent this evil curse?

Is there no relief in sight?
We need to see and hear our son;
you sent us miracles before,
please send us another one.

*My dear wounded children
the pain you feel is real
you have lost a part of yourself
that will take a long time to heal.*

Take each moment as it comes
move to hours and then to days
remembering you are still a family
can cut through the grieving haze.

Find strength in each other
yet find space for yourself to grieve
you all desperately need the time
to comprehend and to believe.

Believe he is in a better place
but not totally out of reach
there are many avenues that can provide
peace and give relief.

The miracles do not stop
but in grief they are harder to see
the pain deadens your senses
but they are always there for thee.

Reach out to your son
he is closer than you think
open up your spiritual eyes
and you will find a link.

A path for your healing
and the place you need to be
so you can say good bye
just one more time...
and set his spirit free.

—In Memory of Bradley James Degraw

Third Letter
June 25th, 1988

> My heart is in anguish within me;
> The terrors of death assail me.
> Fear and trembling have beset me;
> Horror has overwhelmed me.
> I said, "Oh, that I had the wings of a dove!
> I would fly away and be at rest.
>
> —Psalm 55: 4-6

June 25th, 1988

My Dear Son,

It has been one year ago this week that we were in Hawaii. I keep playing over and over in my mind our trip to paradise. I remember staying at the Diamond Head Beach Hotel where we sneaked up to the top and looked out over the city of Honolulu. Do you remember how scared you were of getting caught? I remember our first attempt at swimming at that not so nice beach near the hotel where the coral was so sharp, but we were excited to be in Hawaii. We later did stumble onto Waikiki beach and discovered how nice it was. Remember you and Meg getting a ride back in the little bike cart that a man was peddling? Mom and I waited back at the hotel for you.

I think of that sickening helicopter ride that you seemed

to handle so well, despite that nasty tumor in you brain. I remember how you glowed in recognition and love for Walter, the Hawaiian that befriended you. I will never forget how he took you out by yourself snorkeling by the Capt. Cook Monument, while his girlfriend fed the fish from the boat. She was a Hula dancer and how you loved the Hula. You could not seem to get enough of it. I do not know how many shows we saw, but in every show you never missed a minute of it.

I think of you, my son, whenever I think of Hawaii and I think of Hawaii whenever I think of you...without fail. Do you remember the great time we had on the beach lighting the fireworks as you guys chanted like Indians? Then we all went skinny-dipping in the ocean at night. Wow what a blast that was. Crazy parents, huh?

I remember how cold you were at the Jessie Luau and you were wearing my shirt, but when Jesse called you up on the stage you took it off and proudly walked up there like you owned the place, and the last thing you looked like was cold. I get the chills still whenever I hear that song "Kanaka vi vi" that Jessie sang for you.

Kelly, I am so glad you wanted to go out and see Grandma and Grandpa Kuby before you died. We had such a great time out there. We did not do too much except watch movies and go for short walks and eat. Do you remember the old church down the hill that we investigated? I remember how you really were not feeling good when we went trout fishing, but you did it anyway for Grandma. I remember how you liked Grandma's friends because they had cats. I think you were missing Ernie.

I felt so bad for you when you were crying so hard for your mom when we first arrived and you couldn't stop whimpering. Then we started giving you a little bit of the magic morphine medicine that you grew to like. It took away the pains that you could not identify and relaxed you so not as many hot baths were necessary, considering their low water pressure and how long it took to fill the tub.

Remember, we could not find Cocoa Wheat's for love or money, and we invented our own with instant breakfast? That was the last time you saw your Grandma Kuby, She was so glad to have had that time with you. I remember all these times and I am happy that we had them, but I also remember that you were sleeping later and later everyday. I would go in and check on you and listen for your breathing and check your heartbeat. I had no idea when you would be passing over, Kelly. There is no way to prepare for it, no way to know what to expect. These feelings got worse when we returned to that awful townhouse that we called home. I found myself ghoulishly checking on you at night to still see if you were alive. It was such a strange feeling, almost wanting to find you not breathing and have it all over with: your pain and mine.

When we had hope and we were filled with the spirit of survival and confronted every obstacle with a voracious desire to tear it down. There were no obstacles! During that last month that you were here with us, I lost all hope; I knew that it was over and you were returning home. I felt no fear checking on you or had no hopes that you would be alive. I knew death was coming and I almost ashamedly wished that it would just come and be all over with.

My only regret is not talking with you near the end, that you were indeed dying. I truly believe that you knew and from a previous conversation I know you did not want to talk about dying. But I still wanted to talk to you about it and tell you, "Yes, Kelly, you are dying." You were so tired and listless and your breathing was erratic; we were not sure if you would be like this for weeks or not even last the day. We did not think it would be long, but yet really did not know. It hurts me so much when I think of you lying there on the couch fighting for your breath and staring off into the nothingness, so pale, so sad. I thank you for that wonderful smile that you left us with when your spirit left your body. That gave me the sign that you were now with God and your mission was complete.

Kelly I loved you as a son, I loved you as a boy, and I love you as you. But I never realized just how muchhhhh until now. I cannot believe how much it hurts. You remember in **The Never Ending Story** movie there was "**The Nothing.**" Well, when I am not hurting and not in unexpected bouts of normalcy, there is the ever constant, ever heavy nothing. A step out of place; a step out of time. So when the nothing gets to be too much, I remember, this brings the pain of your loss and the loss of your presence and this memory brings in the pain. I welcome it because with it your memory comes. If I cannot have you, then let me have the pain; it is all I have of you now. I cannot bear to walk by your picture sometimes and see nothing. A lot of the time, that is what I see...nothing and I know that helps to keep me in line with the rest of the world, everyday things to do, work, and of course taking care of mom and Meg.

Kelly I miss you and love you so much it is almost a physical concrete thing. At least as heavy as concrete and just as lasting. I dream of the day that we will again see each other when I leave this earth plane, or in my dreams. I thought things would be getting better and not worse. Right at this moment, I do not think I could feel your loss more profound. I want you back here with us! I want to *watch you playing with your stupid Garbage Pail Kid cards, I want to see you teasing the heck out of Emily. I want to see you diving off the diving board. Christ, I want to see you graduate and have girlfriends. I want you!!!!!!!!*

—Dad

This letter to Kelly was written 6 months following his death and I started replaying in my mind all the things we had done. The whole adventure of miracles and magic that took place in Mexico filled my thoughts. Did that all really happen? Did Kelly really sing in Spanish and swallow invisible pills? Did his tumor really disappear? Did we really sell all our belongings and our house and move to San Diego? Did we honestly set up our home as hospice and plan his funeral while he was still alive? These thoughts and more resounded through my head; it all sounded so crazy and unbelievable. But that is what happened, and it changed our lives forever.

You can imagine our pain and frustration when the cancer returned and killed him so quickly. We had experienced a miracle firsthand. Now where was our God? We had been so sure he was cured. Now Kelly's future was gone and my future with him in it was gone. Clinging to the mystery and magic of those days as well as our other journeys now consumed my every waking moment. Reflecting on our recent experiences, what we did and didn't do, brought back his memories, and with it the pain. With that pain a deep fury was also brought to the surface. The *anger* stage of bereavement reared its ugly head and I was mad.

I would lash out at anybody for seemingly minor indiscretions. For a laid back type of guy this took many people by surprise. This was not in my nature and I would always feel horrible afterwards. There were a few exceptions although that gave me pause. It seems when I "blew up" at a stranger that really (*in my estimation*) deserved a tongue lashing, I always felt better following the event. Anger and it's umbrage of frustration needs to be released. Some times I would go out deep into the woods and just scream. One time I went to an abandoned auto junkyard and with crowbar in hand smashed dozens of headlights and windshields. But most of the time I released my rage through my writing. This was evident in the last couple paragraphs in the previous letter and several of the poems that were written around the same time. All which reflect my pain and longing.

Grief fills the room up of my absent child,
Lies in his bed, walks up and down with me,
Puts on his pretty looks, repeats his words,
Remembers me of all his gracious parts,
Stuffs out his vacant garments with his form.

—William Shakespeare

MAHALO SWEET HAWAII

Hawaii, land of sun and land of love
you call to me upon the breeze
to come and heal my son.

The rainbow ore the falls
scents of Plumeria thick in the air
you call to me so gently
in my dark despair.

Sending messages of healing
of faith, hope and magic
with an awareness of God's presence
in a situation so tragic.

The pounding of the surf
and the swaying of the palm
massages mind and soul
with a tropical spiritual balm.

The warmth of the "Aloha"
the Hawaiian natural way
bathes the soul with healing
and troubles melt away.

The dawning of each new day
brings miracles in motion
with its warm tropic breezes
and salty smell of its ocean.

I pray to God every day
this healing will last
that Hawaii's magical blessing
will heal the hurts of past.

That my son will see the day
when we can make our return
to Hawaii and her islands
and the future that we yearn

Mahalo sweet Hawaii
your touch I'll not forget
the magic of your people
we are forever in you debt.

GRACIAS A DIOS

Mexico you are a mystery, I'm not sure you will ever know
what kind of experience on us you did bestow.
We came here with open hearts as God lead the way;
leading us to our healing and our companion every day.

With your love and great goodness you brought hope to our door
bringing magic and compassion like never seen before.
We were brought down to reality, there was no time to waste
there were many things to be done and to do them in haste.

Kelly's body had to be restored, his energies increased,
many people were brought our way with what they had to teach.
They taught us of logic in the body's natural way
of healing it's intrusions the beset us everyday.

Restore the vital energies that medicines had absorbed
eating only natural food with a stronger faith in our Lord.
God had spoken to us and said our son was made whole;
that his healing was complete, and we had reached our prayed for goal.

Instead of putting our son out to pasture and letting life take it's course
we put our faith back in God, the power and the source.
Sometimes we tend to forget that God has set a plan
a course for all humanity, every woman and every man.

The course is never rigid, He helps us all the way,
we have to look for his guidance, giving thanks when we pray.
There is much power in collective prayer when their energies combine.
Sending waves of healing light down God's own power line.

We have received God's love through his sons and his daughters,
from the flora of the land, and its cleansing healing waters.
God has given back my son for he has many things to do
spreading the word of God's kindness....telling them of you.

HELPLESS TO THE MEMORIES

Oh son, I miss you so with those hypnotic eyes of blue,
I long to hold you in my arms the way I use to do.
I crave to smell again the natural odor distinct to you
imprinted in my olfactory memory from the day that you were new.

I can still hear you giggle with that mischievous glint in your eye
squeezing the hell out of your hamsters or making your sister cry.
Swearing like a sailor with many things that you said
and how you loved to read the books that were stacked beside your bed.

Playing with your Garbage Pail Kid Cards for hours on end
collecting every series they had with every dime that you could spend.
A day does not go by that I do not ruminate over my son
and I reflect upon my tragic loss and all the things that we had done.

I remember when this all began on that Sunday you saw double
and we raced to the hospital....we knew that you were in trouble.
Things have never been the same since that frightening day
when we found out you had cancer and our old lives were swept away.

Swept away and gone forever, there was no turning back
the perfect healthy family that we had, its future turning black.
Three brain surgeries later and a long hospital stay
we finally brought you home, how happy we were that day.

You were left very weak and partially paralyzed on one side
confined to a wheelchair, but had not lost your pride.
You were proud to be alive and glad to be at home again
trying to forget the pain and where you had been.

The wheelchair seemed fun at first but the novelty soon grew old
you realized your limitations before you were told.
You wanted badly to walk any way that you could
so with a tripod cane and some assistance you started doing good.

But soon you were embarrassed by the looks from you peers
and threw down the cane and with it your fears.
We watched you shuffle along holding on to the wall
biting onto our lips so afraid that you would fall.

Fall you did a couple of times and it made you very mad
the tears welled up in my eyes, I felt so very bad.
It hurt me to see you struggle so with your body so very weak
but you were so determined with every goal that you would seek.

So walk you finally did with patience, courage and resolve
you overcame your obstacles and recovered from your falls.
You worked very hard with your therapist and did everything she
asked you to do, she cared for you so very much
and wanted to see you get through.

She pushed you pretty hard at times and you would get upset and cry
you were told it was for your own good, but hard to understand the why.
You switched the dominance of you hands now using your left
instead of your right
progressing very rapidly with your determination and your fight.

You wanted so very badly to again ride your bike down the street
but we were so very frightened of that potentially dangerous feat.
The back of your head was still healing, your neck was very stiff
balance and coordination a problem , leaving room for what if...

What if you fell on the sidewalk and hit your sensitive healing head
it wasn't so long ago you couldn't get out of bed.
But ride your bike you did, going round and round the block
your head held high and smiling...riding bike when you could hardly walk.

The neighbors came out of their houses and they all cheered you on
Hip-hip hooray for Kelly Carmody and the victory he had won.
I will never forget that day and that *real* smile on your face
even though we had lost the war, we had won many a race.

I guess that is what hurts so much, to see all your efforts made in vain
all your courage and hard work, all the tears and all the pain.
You should have gotten more time for the steep price that you had paid
experience more of life's happiness and plans that should be made.

That is my biggest regret that we did not have more time to share
with all the sacrifices you had made, it just wasn't fair.
Fair it may not have been but that is what transpired
the miracles had stopped and your time here expired.

I have to get used to the fact that you are really dead
that the life we had is over, except for re-runs in my head.
I am helpless to the memories, the good ones and the bad
that lay so close to the surface and make me feel so sad.

I just cannot get over you; I am not ready to put you away,
so I'll be self indulgent with my pain and think of you everyday.
Yes it hurts so very much, and the pain may last for years
...but the pain is all that I have left, beside my daily tears.

July 26, 1988

Fourth Letter
September 8th, 1988

> Though they go mad they
> shall be sane,
> Though they sink through the sea
> They shall rise again;
> Though lovers be lost, love shall not;
> -And death shall have no dominion.
>   —Dylan Thomas (1936)

September 8th, 1988

My Dearest Son,

I think things are going better for us here at home. Better in comparison to where we have been, I guess is just a matter of intensity. I do not hurt, as deeply as before, or rather, I am not exhibiting as many painful manifestations as I have previously. I still think of you everyday, almost the first thing in the morning and the last thing at night. As before it was almost nonstop thinking about you. There is probably nothing I do that I do not think about the activity in comparisons of with and without you.

This school year and beginning of school for Meagan seems so different without you. Your mother, who loved to shop with you so much and get you ready for school, is taking it pretty hard. You and she loved to go shopping and school was so important to you. Last year it was so strange with you kids starting school in a strange town and strange people. I hope we did not do wrong by you in doing what we did, but it seemed the right thing to do and you did seem strangely content in that school, compared to Meg who didn't like it at all. I am sorry I never picked up your erasures from that school. I remember fighting with the principal to let you ride your bike to school as well as the school nurse over shots for you. Some day we will talk it all over and we shall understand all the reasons and the whys.

Kelly, Meg is now playing T-ball and soccer and I support her and go to her games, but I cannot help feel a world apart from all the other parents and have no ambition to get involved. It makes me feel so sad thinking of all the things that you are missing out on. Even more so it makes me feel sad over missing out on seeing you involved in so many of life's experiences.

I truly do feel on a deeper soul level that you realized this experience was one of your choosing, for you own soul's reasons—just as Jesus chose His path and knew of His certain demise. I am not saying He was ready to go easily but He knew what awaited Him. In the Garden of Gethsemany, He went through His personal turmoil just as you did when you found out your cancer was back. He knew that this was the end of His earthly life, but chose not to fight it anymore. The mission that He had to do was completed while still in the flesh. He did not rush to His death but accepted it as part of the plan. He did not really want to leave His earthly ties but did not resist, as He knew this is what He had chosen and what He had worked His whole life for.

Just as you worked your whole life to accomplish so much, in such little time. You had completed the task your soul had set forth in this life and when you innately knew it was over, you accepted it and went to meet your God. Jesus had personally met you two years earlier, floating above the operating table when He said, "You will be well." He had pulled you from the jaws of death, for your mission was not yet complete. The last two years are still trying to find a place in my reality and someday it will be a great story to move many people. Your life was truly an inspirational one and that is what gives me the strength to accept the unacceptable in human terms—your loss.

The state I am in now is hard to describe, but it is not the horrifying pain of before, but rather a strange indescribable state, which has followed a relatively up period. I am again finding meaning in life and look forward to utilizing all that you have taught me in your short life. My life has been profoundly changed and I am not who I used to be and I have plans for myself to be as good as I can be and help to heal this planet and its' inhabitants.

I thank you for your great sacrifice and I hope I am worthy of carrying on the lamp of your illumination. I still miss you so much, and it hurts very much if I dwell on it; so forgive me if I do not. I still love you with all my heart and soul and I will always be proud that you chose me as your father on this journey.

With you always......Dad

This, the fourth letter, nine months following Kelly's death, reflects a significant milestone in acceptance. By looking into the depth of destiny and recognizing that the flow of the universe is one of continual change, that energy does not dissipate it only changes form. Growing from change is the opportunity we are presented with each and every day of our life. We must seek from life's daily challenges the reasons that we are experiencing them.

When catastrophic change strikes, it is never more important to recognize how we can benefit our life, our family and the world, by experiencing this most difficult challenge. NOTHING can be done to reverse what has happened. Death can be an angel in disguise for those in great pain; for them it is the ultimate cure. For those left behind the only cure for the pain in grief is acceptance.

The key to acceptance of a significant death in your life is to experience the pain—never deny it. Play out the guilt, your shoulda, woulda, couldas, and let it go. We manufacture guilt and punish ourselves for things beyond our real control. We cannot control destiny, yet we can influence destiny by how we react. Every action causes a reaction. We can never change what has transpired, but we can influence what is yet to be. By choosing to go forward and using your pain to help alleviate pain in others, you will find that your pain is relieved in the process.

The heart has its reasons, which reason does not know.
—Blaise Pascal

GOLDEN OPPORTUNITY

Life is so full of pain, yet so full of light
the duality of our existence so apparent in my plight.
I intensely feel the pain of loss that will not go away
no matter how many books I read or hours that I pray.

They say that time heals all things but what else is there to say?
For time marches on, minute after minute, day after day.
There is no magic cure only a slow process of change
as our perceptions of reality grows more lucid and less strange.

The pain never really goes away, a lesson we are cruelly learning
but lies in a state of remission; a glowing ember always burning.
It is in understanding this lesson that we gain some relief
we don't shut out our loved ones life but hold on to our belief.

Our belief that life never really dies and we shall be together again
and understand that this present moment will too have an end.
The only constant we have is change and change is the essence of being
a metamorphic blueprint in flux that we resist our minds from seeing.

Man is resistant to life's modulations forever clinging to the past,
wanting things the way they were
and for the present moment to forever last.
That can never happen, we cannot hold back tomorrow
for the sun will surely rise and with it, pain and impending sorrow.

So we must look for the gift encapsulated in our grief
seek out the potential for growth and what the experience has to teach.
There is no way to change the fact that our loved one has died
no miracle that can bring them back or erase the tears that we have cried.

We must face the cold reality that a part of us is gone forever
the physical evidence of their existence cut from our parental tether.
The awful truth of our loss makes us escape inside
cut off from the rest of the world, a safe place to hide.

And hide we must to endure the pain,
a time to recharge the spirit and not go insane.
But after a period of time we have to break out
or lose touch with the world and what we're about.

We have the golden opportunity to advance our spiritual being
and turn sorrow to joy; a different perspective in our seeing.
Seeing the potential in all life experience that can fortify our soul
bringing us closer to God and the healing of humanity our goal.

To transcend our painful condition that man is reticent to communicate
and make their life a legacy that through our acts can illuminate.
If we can use the energy consumed in our bereavement
and transform it into a tool for our own spiritual achievement.

If we can only give credence to their life;
that there was a reason they chose this path
and that their soul had chosen this direction
and not some vengeful God's wrath.
That we as family were also selected to assist them on their way
players in a greater plan we shall too understand some day.

So we must try to make the best of a clearly unacceptable situation,
and put our self-pity to a rest and grow in spiritual maturation.
Our lives will never be the same without them at our side,
but what a gift they have given us,
their love…that in us will always reside.

IN THE SHADOW OF MY DESPAIR

You have no idea just how I feel
unless you're in my shoes
no way you can comprehend
the depth of sorrow in my blues.

The shock carried me away
when my son first died
a cloud like calm enveloped me
as friends hugged me and we cried.

They then felt the bitter pain
putting themselves in my place
envisioning the loss of their child
as they gazed upon his face.

They at once realized how vulnerable
one can truly be
how painful that reality
was brought clear for them to see.

To see such a beautiful child
laying cold and lifeless in his funeral bier
strikes terror in any parents' heart
that their child could too expire.

Uncomfortable people don't know what to say
so you hear, *"If there is anything that I can do..."*
feeling helpless in a situation
so difficult to get through.

So many people often exclaim,
"I don't know how you do it,
I love my children so awfully much
there is no way I could get through it."
My God! Does this mean because I am calm,
I love my children less?
How else could I handle it,
under such great duress.

God grants us a little time
a short period that we are numb with shock
to attend to funereal arrangements
and the ability to even talk.

It is when the wake is over
the funeral said and done
the graveside interment finished
or the ashes scattered in the sun.

These acts of life's finality
start to erode the facade of calm
and the reality of my great loss
breaks down God's numbing balm.

It is said that grief takes time
at least two years most experts agree
before a semblance of normalcy
will start to return to me.

At times I feel quite normal
in fact almost good
and then the boom is lowered
as I expected that it would.

Intense pain then returns
and racks my very soul
depression I have never know before
starts to take its toll.

The real world fades away…
people talk and are not heard
apathy surrounds my being
it's difficult to utter a word.

Tears flow in a sudden flood
with deep convulsive groans
wails of torment escape my throat
that vibrates from my bones.
As an exhausted shell of myself
I feel washed out and spent
the intensity diminishing
from this scenario of my lament.

I slowly then recover
and feeling better in part
it seems a great weight has been lifted
temporarily from my heart.

It is these intense feelings
other people do not perceive,
not realizing the profundity of pain
that each day I do receive.

Their lives go on as before
with a modicum of change
their petty priorities seem unimportant
that in their lives they do arrange.

I have a lowered tolerance
for trivial problems that people exclaim
no time for their trifling complaints
or who won the baseball game.

I understand that it is my perception
it is no fault of their own
but I cannot help the way I'm feeling
caught in this "grieving zone."

I wonder how long it will take
before I lose a friend
because of my intolerant moods
that could put a friendship to end.

I think that friends that truly care
will always be by my side
and in the shadow of my despair
their love will still reside.

It may take several years
before I can stand tall again
and I will thank God for the loving arms
of the people I still call a friend.

O Death the healer, scorn thou not, I pray
To come to me: of cureless ills
thou art the one physician.
Pain lays not its touch upon a corpse.
                    —Aeschylus (456 B.C.)

Fifth Letter
October 31st, 1988

Hearts that are united through the medium of sorrow,
Will not be separated by the glory of happiness.
Love that is cleansed by tears will remain eternally pure and beautiful…
— Kahil Gibran

October 31st, 1988

My Dearest Son,

Here it is Halloween again, your holiday of all holidays, but this year it is not the same and it will be quite awhile before it ever is again. I remember how excited you would get and how you would talk about your new costume months before Halloween; those years in Bayport, when things were normal and you were well. You and your buddy Jason would hit the streets, bags in hand…ahhhh, those were the days.

Last year I was in California all by myself, while you, Meg and your mom were back in Minnesota making the rounds of your last Halloween. Your mom told me how you crawled up to a few doors because you were too weak to walk. It breaks my heart to think about it, but it showed your determination and priorities.

Kelly, it has been a roller coaster of emotions since you died. I thought it was getting better; then two weeks ago the bottom fell out of my reality and I lapsed into a period of deep depression. I called in sick to work, as I was truly out of it. I immersed myself into you for days. I watched all the home movies/videos and looked at photos and I cried. I miss you so much that I tried to occupy my thoughts with busy activities or deaden the pain with alcohol. At times I feel like a wounded dog running away for his pain and being unable to, I finally collapse into an exhausted heap.

This last spell was by far the worst and lasted almost a week. I know it will not be the last, but God help me, it wiped me out. When I came out of it, I felt much better and still feel good, except for the fact now of Halloween. With your upcoming birthday, death day, and Christmas I feel very vulnerable. I feel so confused trying to sort it all out and maintain a normal life. It is hard to feel normal when every thought or action that I have is filtered through the grieving me. Every quark of my being is in grief.

All input is only relevant as it is seen without you. It's like seeing life on a television screen that has severe weather warnings flashing constantly on the bottom of the screen: "WARNING! KELLY IS DEAD. HOW CAN YOU VIEW THE WORLD NORMALLY WITH THIS KNOWLEDGE?" Right now it feels as if this storm warning will be with me the rest of my life; at this point, I just don't know. I thought I had all the answers in dealing with death and dying, but I found out there really are no pat answers. Some day I will join you and then, I too, shall know.

Remember when I asked you to give me a sign this spring of something new growing in our yard? Thank you for responding with the three cornstalks. I know it was you that sent them. Three cornstalks growing right out of the lawn, now that is quite a trick !!! I think the first stalk represented the birth and death of your life before cancer. The second stalk, the symbol of your healing and your ultimate physical death. The third stalk survived and bore three ears of corn that bore the fruits of seeds you had sown. The first two corn stalks died as did your body and mind. The third lived and bore fruit as your spirit also lives and is now bearing fruit for all to see. One ear was for Meg, one ear for your mom, and one for me. We shall treasure them. It is also interesting to let you know that Meg came home with a book from the school library called **The Three Corn Stalks.** The book indicates that the three stalks are an ancient sacred symbol for Mexico. I thought the reason you chose the cornstalks had something to do with Mexico.

I promised you that I would quit smoking last January 1st and I did. I feel that was another gift from you. You are no longer here in the physical, but you continue to affect change in my life. So in my mind, part of you is still very much alive, more than just the eternal spirit living on aspect, but a real living spark of who you are, still lives on in my soul. This is whom I am writing to.

Your legacy is also alive and growing and some day I shall finish the book of your life and our adventure. It will give to the world an example of what great love and faith in God can do. I am proud to be a small part in bringing it to the world. Through your struggle and suffering others shall find hope and in finding hope, find and know their God. I thank you again for choosing me as your dad, that fact alone helps me bear the pain and continue on with my life. Together we shall spread the word, as was prophesied last summer in Mexico.

I love you and miss you desperately. I long for your touch that I cannot do a damn thing about, which is so painfully frustrating. As I was tickling Meg last night, I tried to remember the last time I actually tickled you and you laughed a deep hearty child's laugh. It was a long time ago. You had to grow up so fast and give up so much before you ever left us physically; for that I am sorry. This path was your choice, just as Jesus chose his path. The sufferings known here on earth are nothing compared to the great joy that you are now experiencing in the bosom of our God. Until I write again....its hello and not good-bye.

—Dad

This letter was written on Halloween night, eleven months after Kelly's death. It vividly reflects the roller coaster of emotions that one can experience in the process of their grief. Special days and holidays are especially difficult when those days approach and it is the first year without your loved one. Last year they were still alive and together you were making memories of every special moment for the last time. This year they are but a memory.

There will be times that you will want to immerse yourself into the memories and feel the pain. Recognize the pain and the emotions that come with it, allow it all in. Bittersweet emotions will well up and you will feel vulnerable and alone. This can be difficult, but it is very therapeutic as it allows vivid recollections involving all of your senses. In this space and time you become very close to your loved one and can actually feel the closeness of their spirit. This is the joy that lays beneath the pain, the gift in the grief, a taste of their life be it ever so brief. Do not put away their memories forever, let them help heal and nourish your spirit. As Frederic Nietzsche said: *"That which does not kill me, makes me strong."*

Take a chance. It may be difficult and exhausting but it's worth the price. You get so much back and it can actually be a stimulus for your healing. Be open to signs from your loved one;

it is at these especially painful times that they reach out to us in our need. It may be a song on the radio, a bird at the windowsill, their scent on the wind, or a very vivid dream; a seemingly insignificant random event occurring at just the right time.

This letter is again about total acceptance. About hitting the nadir of pain and depression by immersing yourself into the pain. Feeling it all, then slowly getting up and accepting the future, as it is, your life without them—they are dead. Our family, our jobs, the world, needs us back with them. We have to continue on with our good works that we have yet manifest and pursue the path that God has set before us. We will be provided with the strength when we need it the most. We have many lives that we have yet to influence, hearts to touch and souls that need to connect. This is our destiny and we have to play it out and grow from it, however it presents itself.

Look for the design in our experiences that can influence our choices in the future. There are no accidents, no mistakes, and no poor choices; only acceptance of *all* the choices you have made. The magic of it is…we always have choices—and it's always the right choice for us. This may be difficult to understand soon after experiencing the affects of a perceived poor choice (real or imagined), but it is those affects that we experience which pave the way to our future. Pitfalls can be windfalls, roadblocks can be stepping-stones and the Y in the road will always rise up to meet us

Our destiny exercises its influence over us even when, as yet, we have not learned its nature: it is our future that lays down the law of our today.
—Friedrich Nietzsche

FOOTSTEPS THROUGH THE VALLEY OF THE
SHADOW OF DEATH

Yea as I walk through the valley of the shadow of death
bearing the burden of grief upon my back.
The valley is dark, deep and suffocating—
I long for the fresh air that I lack.

The journey into the valley is a lonely one,
neither is it night, nor is it day,
it is not hot and dry, cold and wet
only different shades of gray.

The walls of the valley are spongy and thick
they seem to absorb all sound.
The floor has a great gravitational pull
making it difficult to get around.

Time stands still in this awful place
a direction is hard to find;
one wanders aimlessly about
in a dreamlike state of mind.

The air is dense and viscous
almost liquid as it surrounds your being.
When you try to reach out to a friend
it occludes your eyes from seeing.

It seems there is no escape,
no possible place to run.
You long to find an open door
that will again let in the sun.

You raise your hands up to God
to beseech him for a healing.
Begging Him to take away your pain
And the emotions you are feeling.

Your supplications seem to fall on deaf ears,
God apparently is not around.
Maybe he is off helping others
unaware of your lamenting sounds.

It is now that you really need Him
to rescue you from this desolate concavity.
Craving the comfort of his embrace
and away from death's depravity.

Where is my God; now tell me;
why is there no answer to my call?
have years of faith deserted me
now that my back is to the wall?

I know that death is our greatest reward
the overlying reality that is in store.
Knowing that death is a but a mere transition
an altered state but yet so much more.

This is, of course, the Nirvana of Heavenly glory
for those who leave the human plane
But does little for the survivors
that are left alone and racked with pain.

For we are the ones who are left to die
in the valley of the shadow of death
To perish when our day too will come
and we draw our final breath.

It may seem that God has forsaken us
as we travel alone in this canyon of despair
—But it is then that he carries us
and was and will always be there.

It is just that in our pain
it is hard to feel His hand.
So He carries us ever so gently
until again we can finally stand.

Stand up to the stark reality
of the loss that we have to bear.
Realizing we must live our lives to the fullest
with the love we have yet to share.

So if you feel God has abandoned you
in the depths of your deepest sorrow.
Remember God always listens,
and will be there for you tomorrow.

SOUL TALK

As I live my life, I see, hear, and feel things
which is all for the soul purpose of me experiencing this life.
My mission in *this* life is to try to live to the fullest.
To learn and understand my deck of cards that lay out before me to play.
There will be good cards and there will be bad, both of which I will
have to deal with.

I believe God has sent me on this journey to teach me lessons of
which I have not yet acknowledged from my past lives.
I will try to understand everything that God will allow my soul to learn.
So far my journey has been about understanding loss and the grief
of losing a loved one,
how you find your inner strength to help you accept
how death can be beautiful if you let it.

I have learned of pain and suffering of war and how cruel people
can be to each other.
If only people would listen to their souls and look into their dreams.
I know love can overcome everything in life no matter what the situation.

I am the protector of my family in this lifetime.
I'm here to be their strength and the sole core
which holds these two beautiful people together.
God gave me that gift.

I truly believe that I was born
by this couple to help guide them through their life as they are
helping me get to know and experience my life as a beautiful thing
—and how love can overcome...Everything.

—Meagan Carmody (Kelly's sister)
written at age 12

Oh, call my brother back to me!
I cannot play alone:
The summer comes with flower and bee…
Where is my brother gone?
—Felicia Dorthea Hemans

Sixth Letter
December 25th, 1988

Things do not change; we change.
—Henry Thoreau
Walden (1854)

December 25th, 1988

Dear Kelly,

Well, today is Christmas Day, and it is just not the same without you. I love Christmas songs and the general atmosphere of Christmas, but now that it is here I feel quite miserable and miss you more than ever. It is important that we keep our chins up for Meagan because Christmas is for kids after all. But this is a chore!!!! I feel so tired and it is not just the midnight shift. My throat has a lump in it that seems worse on that shift, when I am so tired. The doctor says it is stress and recommended Valium. I refuse to be put on Valium forever so I will try to live with it and keep my stress level down. Maybe all my losses have finally caught up to me, with your loss being the straw that broke the camel's back. Sometimes I wish the world would stop and let me off. How long am I going to feel this way? There are worse disasters, more carnage in the world than I have experienced. Why can't I feel better when I rationalize this way? Remember last February when I asked you for a sign

growing in the yard this spring? I never in my wildest
dreams thought that you could orchestrate such a profound
message as you did. Yes, I found the three cornstalks growing
in the yard. I understand they represent the healing that
took place in Mexico. I was happy with just the presence of
the cornstalks, but ecstatic and overjoyed with the message
you sent to that last ear of corn on December 1, with the one
word "DAD" written in the husk with corn mold for
ink...Wow! How astounding! I lived on that for weeks.

I am sure you saw how we were on the anniversary of
your death. I have never cried so much and so hard in my
life. I cannot believe how much it hurt that day. I guess I
fully realized that you were dead and let myself truly feel
that all day long. I know now it is going to take a long, long
time to heal. I never knew I could love somebody so much. I
have never known depression before or had any stress related
illness. I understand that by the nature of things I will get
better, but maybe I don't want to just yet. I just do not know!

I know that the holidays would be rough and we shall
see how we recover. Thank you for the energy that you
expended to get back to me. I will love you all the rest of my
days. When you have the strength, please give Dustin a visit.
He is hurting pretty bad still. I will try to help from this
end. . . Always loving you my dear, sweet son.

—Dad

This sixth letter clearly illustrates the pain and sadness
experienced during the holidays and the anniversary date.
Conversely it also reflects the joy that is received from miracles
of the spirit, undying love, and faith.

As I wrote in this letter, I was experiencing physical symptoms from my grief. The pain on his death day anniversary date was extreme and profound. We opened his trunk of things containing drawings, toys, books, *Garbage Pail Kid* cards, the blanket he died in, and lots of nine-year-old boy stuff. We immersed ourselves into the pain and cried deep, wailing and painful tears.

In the first letter, I had asked Kelly to get back to somebody with the code word. When Kelly was still alive his mom had talked to Kelly about dying and together they had come up with a "code word." Kelly promised her that if he died he would get back to her with their code word. After we had gone through all the stuff in Kelly's trunk and we were putting things back, we found an old notebook in a pile of his magazines. It looked unused with little or no writing in it, but when we were putting it back into the trunk it fell open to one page with a single drawing on it. The drawing was one of those simple kid drawings where you trace out your hand and make a turkey and it had the letters of Kelly's name on each finger. The code word had been "Turkey." Another coincidence, maybe, but we knew better and our spirits were again lifted. We were emotionally spent and exhausted; yet buoyed with gifts from the spirit.

At that time, I was experiencing some tightness in my throat, which felt like a huge lump, making it difficult to swallow. My doctor could find nothing physically wrong and thought it might be stress related (imagine that). I quit drinking coffee and tried to reduce other stressors in my life. The doctor now wanted to try Valium, but I did not want to medicate my pain. The reason for the pain, I believed, was from my current horrific grief on top of old unexpressed grief that needed to be released.

I now sought a more holistic approach, and with the *New Age* thinking paradigm shift in full swing, there were many avenues to explore. I had experienced the Rebirthing Process for the first time when we were in California and was impressed with its results. I searched locally and soon found a lady that practiced out of her home in Wisconsin. I thought if I went back to day one, I might find some clue to help me now. I made an appointment since the throat thing was driving me crazy.

I drove to her house in rural Wisconsin with cautious optimism. The woman was very earthy (people I chidingly call *granola eaters*) and in her late fifties. The house was quiet with no one else apparently there. She took my coat and hat and brought me down to her studio in the basement. She had me lie down on a couch while she sat next to me on a hardback chair holding my hand. She slowly explained to me about rebirthing and what I was to expect. I was told to breathe very slowly and to relax, clear my mind and concentrate only on my breathing. As I was getting my rhythm down she explained that I may or may not go back to the day of my birth. What happens is what is supposed to happen for you and this could mean going back to any significant event in your life.

I kept up my rhythmic breathing as she sat quietly by my side, coaching occasionally when my rhythm would stray. I then heard the furnace kick on in the next room and I was immediately launched back to the day my father died. I was fourteen years old in my bed in a basement room next to the furnace. It was early morning and I had to get up to get ready for the county fair to exhibit my dog for a 4-H project. My father was in the hospital recovering from triple bypass surgery, my mother, who had been there all night, had just gotten home. She called me upstairs and said, "Son, you are the man of the family now. Your father has died and we need to tell your sisters."

I then started to cry harder and harder and then screamed loudly, "NO!!!" at the top of my lungs, probably scaring the wits out of this poor lady. Her gentle touch and soothing voice brought me back to reality. I was back in *her* basement on her couch, the pillow wet with tears and a throat that was really sore now. I tried to regain my composure, it was as if I had suddenly awakened from a very vivid dream. The epiphany then hit me and I realized that I was never allowed to grieve for my father. My mother's words, "You are the man of the house now," came back to me. I then understood what I had done at such a young age. I took on the role. I was the man of the house and took care of what needed to be done. There was no more grieving; I solicitously put it away and took care of the house, the farmyard, my mom and my sisters.

I left rural Wisconsin that day feeling weird, tired, apathetic, sad, depressed, with a sore throat worse then when I had arrived. My head was filled with thoughts of my father— everything about him. I could even smell his scent right there in the car. Most of these strong recollections faded within a few days and, to my delight, so did the lump in my throat. I surmised that before I could adequately deal with my present grief and pain for my son, I had to go back and deal with the unresolved grief for my father. It worked!

As I stated earlier there was a miracle of the spirit that happened on Kelly's death day anniversary: the miracle of the cornstalks. These miracles happen all around us everyday, all the time. It is our perception and our faith that allows us to see them. You do not have to be a psychic, clairvoyant or clerical leader to experience these phenomena; the ability lies within us all and is closer to the surface than you think. Participating in a miracle also has an analgesic affect that helps heal the spirit in the process of bereavement. When I had asked my son for a sign from the grave that he was doing fine, I never dreamt of something so profound and miraculous could happen. The poem that follows this writing tells the story, but suffice it to say, it was a miracle. This for me was when the true healing began, bringing with it acceptance and letting go.

The Miracles of the Church seem to me to rest not so much upon faces of or voices or healing power coming suddenly near to us from afar off, but upon our perceptions being made finer, so that for a moment our eyes can see and or ears can hear what is there about us always.

—Willa Sibert Cather

THE THREE CORNSTALKS

In December of last year
my young son passed away
I wanted proof that he survived
so I would talk, when I did pray.

I asked him for a sign
that would grow in our yard this spring
not a timely rainbow
or a bird on a wing.

I requested a living indication
that Kelly would manifest
growing from God's green earth
a portent at my request.

That summer we had a drought
the ground as dry as bone
but yet from the parched & dried up lawn
three plants grew all alone.

Three corn stalks grew
where none had grown before
no seeds were ever planted
amongst the weeds galore.

These three corn stalks formed a triangle
its terminus pointing southwest
toward the land of Kelly's healing
and the miracle that we knew best

Later in the summer
the northwest corn stalk withered and bent
like the loss of Kelly's childhood
before his life was spent.

A few weeks later
the northeast corn stalk died
just as Kelly's physical body had
where his soul had chosen to reside.

The last corn stalk survived
and bore fruit for all to see
a sacred symbol of Mexico
are the corn stalks three.

This year on the first of December
a mourning dove sat at our door
beseeching us to watch her
for the message that she bore.

This bird captivated us
as she hopped across the lawn
then flew over the lone corn stalk
and in a moment... was gone.

I trudged through the snowy yard
anticipation thick in the air
my intuitive senses reeling
in hopes of what could be there.

I examined the dried and withered stalk
for a message it might contain
and near the bottom nearly covered with snow
one last ear did remain.

I plucked this last and lonely ear
pulling its yellowed husk slowly back
within I found a tiny cob
with mold of green and black

This putrefaction of the cob
imprinted a word that could be read
stained clearly on the yellow husk
the word "DAD" was all it said.

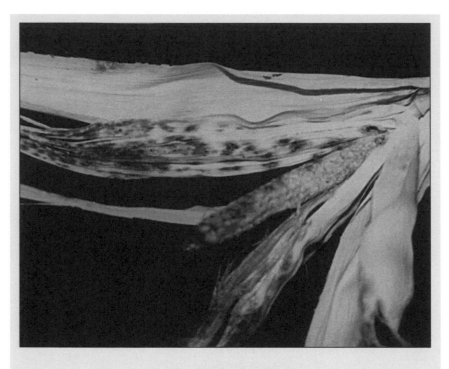

—actual photo (1987)

To... **DAD**

—From Kelly

LOVE ME, NEVER LEAVE ME

My God I need your presence
like I never have before
my healing is slow an painful
with memories behind every door.

This time of year
will never be the same
for my family and for the many friends
of my dear son who was slain.

The summer is beginning
young graduates are everywhere
Tunes of Pomp and circumstance
ring loudly in the air.

Commencement ceremonies carry on
as my tears flow in streams
proud parents unaware
of my pain of unrealized dreams.

Unware of my inner pain
that sears the soul in grief
mourning for the life of my son
whose time here was much too brief.

His physical life was removed
stolen from me in his prime
never to know his kiss again
or feel his love sublime.

I feel so damn cheated
A deep sadness covers my heart
please let the time pass quickly
and I can make another start.

Start my second year of healing
learning to live again
to climb through this fog of sorrow
and where my life has been.

I forgive my son for dying
I will let his spirit fly
release the anger still in my heart
no longer asking why.

I know there are no answers
that I can and will endorse
my life goals have now been changed
on a totally different course.

I know not where I am going
so God please lead the way
help me again find the strength
to greet another day.

Hold on to me dear Lord
wrap me in your loving arms
I feel so alone and helpless
life has lost all its charms.

I know countless others
who have also endured this pain
their sons and daughters lost in war
or cancerous cells gone insane.

No matter when our children are taken
it will always be unfair
when they depart this earth before us
and leave us in dark despair.

So grant me Lord
those special moments that only you can give
that can alleviate my sorrow
and I can begin again to live.

To live my life in it's altered course
and do the things that I can
just being able to function at all
is proof that you have a plan.

So God, love me never leave me
I need you everyday
I feel your loving presence
whenever I sit and pray.

And when I pray to you my Lord
I feel Kelly's presence in my heart
thank you for that gift
and the peace that it imparts.

Seventh and Last Letter
April 2nd, 1989

I have no pain, dear mother, now;
But oh! I am so dry:
Just moisten my poor lips once more;
And, mother, do not cry!

— Edward Farmer

April 2nd, 1989

My Dearest Son,
 I have not written for quite awhile, but I think that means I am doing better. The signs that you have given us have been truly miraculous and I share them with many people. When you sent the five doves when I was reading the poem "Letting Go" to your mother was awesome! You know me well enough to find out what the significance of the Number five was. I talked to a lady at church who was a numerologist and she said it meant, "letting go!!!" My God that says it all.
 I take that sign as a mutual letting go as we release each other to move on. I still would like to hear from you now and then although. I would really like to have a heart to heart talk with you as visually as you can make it (or I can make it) or better yet as we can both make it in my dreams. I need one good last hug from you that will last me for the rest of my life. I miss you so much!!!!! I miss you like

you have just gone away and my heart aches at certain times that just pop up. It is not the intense pain that it was. There is the pain of separation, being away from you physically. Then there is the pain of separation itself, the actual act of separation that was so intense and painful. That separation has finally reached its breaking point and the separation has taken place. Now it is just the ache of our being separated and not the extreme pain of the separation process.

Just as your mother raised you for nine months inside her womb, nurturing you and protecting you, she then had to give you up after the ninth month. She had to separate from you physically and it was very painful, that act of separation. She then suffered later after she recovered with the ache of that separation. She no longer was physically responsible for your life, and she felt the loss of the ultimate maternal feeling of having you inside of her and grieved that. Now after nurturing you and being responsible for you for nine years, she then had to give you up again, and with it came that terrible pain of separation. The whole separation scenario played over again. Only this time, you are now born into a new life that is a more permanent separation. There is no physical contact. It maybe a quick return for you, but a long wait for us until we can see you again.

Our return to Mexico was of great importance for us all. It gave us an opportunity to let go and carry on with our personal destinies. We cannot change the facts of our separation so we must make the best of where we are now. For a while, I just wanted to die and join you, while selfishly ignoring all the responsibilities I have here, especially for your sister. I also now realize what a great legacy you left us with, and I would be renege in my duty not to carry on the work that you had started. The work and purpose of your lifetime was the main reason that we were picked as your parents by you. You picked us to help in the task set before you and to carry on with your work and the work of our Lord's that now seems so synonymous in their natures.

If I was to give up and become an emotional cripple and let the pain of separation maim me for life, I would be doing you such a great disservice and make your life of great trials and tribulations all for naught. I must and will spread the word of God and what faith in him can do and I shall do it my son, with your life. Not many people have done as much with their life at full measure as you have done already with your few short years on this earth. We will continue on with our path that you have started for us. I feel more abundant in the spirit then ever before in my life. You've given that to me, Kelly, and I thank you. I want to be of service to mankind and my God more than ever before.

I would give it all up in a heart beat if I could only have you back here with us, but that can never be so I will expand upon all that we have learned in the school that was your life. I will help to heal mankind as best as I can and spread the word of the faith that can produce miracles. You will always be an active part of my life and together we shall turn my sorrow into joy. Please continue to be that light that guides me and keeps my spirit alive and let me be a conduit of healing energy.

As man suffers at the thought of the crucifixion of Christ, and yet without that reality that he knew was his destiny, where would the world be today? Just as you did, knowing your destiny would create a living testimony of faith. We suffer at our loss, but rejoice in the glory that is your spirit.

I love you, Dad

This was the last letter that I had penned to my son, some fifteen months down the road following his death. It was then that I finally accepted the fact that he was really dead. Part of that acceptance had to deal with a trip back to Mexico. My wife thought it was crazy but she acquiesced at my insistence that it was something we needed to do.

So much magic happened in Mexico and we as a family were buoyed up spiritually from the whole experience. Now a year and some months following his death I had to go back to Mexico and see if it had all been real. The memory of it all seemed like some vivid dream that I could not let go of. Return we did, only to find a whole different landscape.

The beach house where we had stayed for several months had burned to the ground. Nothing remained. We went to the chapel where the healing had taken place. Dona Nieves, who owned the chapel, was in Mexico City for an extended stay so was not available. The Medium (Maria) had not been around for quite some time we were told. We did not meet any of the friends that we had made and we were even hassled by the local police.

When we had been there before, we were treated like gods and everyday was a good day. It was as if it had all been a dream, like a *Brigadoon* experience that was there for a short time, only to vanish again. We drove that day out of Mexico with very mixed emotions. We knew the miracles had happened. How could it have all changed so much? What does this all mean?

We flew home and when the plane pulled onto the runway and up to the terminal, I received my answer. I could see my wife's parents in the window holding the hand of our daughter Meagan. It was then that I realized that she was all I had left. She deserved all of me. As I stared at Meagan, I had a vision, a mental image of my son's face on a large kite in the vast blue sky. His eyes were alive, happy and brilliantly blue as the sky around him. His smile was one of peace, contentment, and self realized assuredness. Gazing into his eyes once more I found myself lost in a reverie of pure joy. With tears streaming down my face and totally unaware of my surroundings, I saw myself clutching desperately to the string that connected to the kite. It was then that I realized how extremely tight I was holding on to the string. I was so afraid of letting it go.

Momentarily, my connection to the outside world returned and as if looking through a tunnel I stared at my darling daughter behind the thick safety glass. I then knew I had to make a choice to let go of my son and give all my energy to my daughter, who was alive and needed me so much. It was painful for me to do, but as I slowly walked up the ramp to my awaiting daughter, I unclenched my hand and let go of the kite string. The kite never strayed, but remained high in the azure sky and my son smiled down at me as if to say, "Now that was n't too hard was it, Dad?" My daughter was now running down the ramp and soon was wrapping her arms around me. I scooped her up in an instant holding her very tight. I gave Kelly a wink and the vision fading I covered my daughter with tender kisses. It felt good to come home.

From wind to wind, earth has one tale to tell;
All other sounds are dulled, and drowned, and lost,
In this one cry "farewell."

—Celia Laighton Thaxter

LETTING GO...

We embraced a miracle
that not long ago cured our son
his malignant brain tumor disappeared
and we no longer had to run.

We had traveled down to Mexico
after two weeks in the Hawaiian Isles
with the enchantment of that paradise
still evident in our smiles.

My son was feeling better
our daughter was having a ball
my wife and I just happy
to be away from it all.

To be away from our jobs
no television, movies or phones
no well meaning surprise visits
we were very much alone.

We ate up the sun and beach
consumed healthy foods everyday
as a family we were truly one
giving thanks to God as we pray.

In this little Mexican village
we were guided to a chapel
and the Lord spoke to us of a healing
without radiation, drugs or scalpel.

Jesus announced through this old woman
that our son would be healed
with diet, lots of faith and a little magic
his death sentence could be repealed.

Raw eggs still in the shell
were rubbed upon his head
surgery in pantomime performed
by a doctor who was dead.

A doctor who in spirit
dispensed medications from thin air
changing spiritual bandages daily
we believed that he was there.

My son could see and feel
the invisible pills he was asked to take
we felt the presence of the Lord
with each appearance He would make.

It was spoken that he would be well
in just six weeks time
we followed the spiritual instructions
in hopes that he would be fine.

My son started singing in fluent Spanish
an ancient hymn out the blue
sung in harmony with the Mexican locals
—it was then that we knew.

Knew that God had lead us here
to this remote little town
being co-workers in a miracle
in an experience so profound.

We put our lives on hold
as a family we were together
we put all our faith in God
and enjoyed the beach and sunny weather.

The real world had stopped
and we gladly got off for awhile
to totally work on our son's healing
and again see his radiant smile.

Our son's strength progressively returned
he could run and swim again
we could see him change before our very eyes
from the sick boy he had been.

In the little chapel it was said my son was healed
take him back to your doctors at home
and prove to them what God has done
with the faith that you have shown.

The Doctors were totally shocked
the could not believe their eyes
the MRI scan showed no tumor
that previously was baseball size.

We danced on air that day
with smiles that couldn't fade
the greatest feeling in all my life
the sweetest victory ever made.

Circumstances changed in the months that followed
and dark clouds returned our way
my son's cancer spread like fire
our victory was turning gray.

My boy's spirit left his body
his physical journey here ended
to join with his God & maker
on whose miracle we had depended.

We put our faith in God
and He allowed the final healing
I was grateful for my son's peace
but hard to comprehend the pain that I was feeling.

The extreme pain lasted a long time
I grieved so very hard
still crying in anguish a year later
or whenever I was caught off guard.

My wife and I decided to return
to Mexico and it's magic
say good-by to all that it held
and the joy that turned so tragic.

The beach home where we had stayed
had mysteriously burned to the ground
the homes on either side
left unscathed and standing sound.

The chapel was quiet and empty
our hearts were filled with sadness
had the miracle really happened
or was this all sheer madness ?

I was as if though
we were never there
just a little village in Mexico
with the smell of salt sea air.

We had lived a Brigadoon existence
the reality is what we made it
the miracle could have happened anywhere
on any stage that we had played it.

There is no going back
what was, will never be
we had been blessed by God
and now what was...is free.

When the plane landed on the runway
I could feel my daughter's heart
through the hard steel and heavy glass
I felt the love it did impart.

I knew right at that moment
she was our whole family now
a new life built for her
that we will endorse and allow.

When my son went to spirit
I held his soul like a kite
afraid to let go of the silver string
lest his soul would soar out of sight.

In my mind, I let go of that string
his face still smiling down at me
it was in the letting go
that set my spirit free.

My son will always be there
I did not need to hold on so tight
now I can grasp on to other things
and still behold his loving light.

We experienced a powerful miracle
feeling God's love in manifest
something I shall remember always
but yet can put to rest.

Be put to rest as my past
but still be shared will all
giving a legacy to his life
as he answered to his call.

I loved my son very dearly
and miss him with all my heart
but by letting him move on
my new journey will begin to start.

—a new beginning
March 3, 1989

FOLLOWING YOUR BLISS THROUGH DESPAIR

Why am I surrounded in pain that others never see;
some people seem protected from harm
why then not me?

One trauma after another
has burgeoned out the blue
surrounding my life in sorrow
what am I to do?

My pain seems non-ending
peace and happiness is conceptual and abstract
goals and plans for the future
seem atrophied and black.

Everyday is a constant struggle
my God what have I done?
how have I offended thee
that you block out all my sun?

Have I done something so bloody wrong
that I am being punished for this way?
Are you a God of vengeance
that makes his children pay?

No, I cannot believe that of my God
for He has been there by my side
always compassionate to my needs
in the many hours that I have cried.

God does not mete out pain
he only delivers love & light
the distress and sorrow that we feel
are all a part of life.

We have chosen a certain path
we may not consciously be aware
selected the avenue that is right for us
despite its dark despair.

Our decision does not create misfortune
life is a tragedy waiting to unfold
but being aware of our greater purpose
is the alchemy that turns lead to gold.

The minutes, hours, and days pass by
like the river that flows to the sea
what was the present moment
again will never be.

So when the woes of tragedy come our way
and death rears its ugly head
one must confront the fact of life
that our loved one is truly dead.

There is no way to bring them back
the facts are as cold as ice
what has happened is the bitter truth
that no rational can suffice.

Life again will bloom for you
it will not always be this bleak
know in your heart there is a greater good
that has yet to reach its peak.

For those whose paths are filled with hurt
more than their fair share
will gain much more from this life
if they keep their hearts aware.

Happiness will again be yours
a healing will take place
you will recognize your destiny
that you can and will embrace.

It is in recognition of life's kismet
with its portents along the way
that you can find your key to bliss
and find joy in every day.

In the discovery that life has direction
beyond your conscious thought
that divine guidance is always there
whether its cognizant or not.

Destiny is not cast in stone
it can be up or down the hill
the decision with your options
are choices of your free will.

Assess the commonalties in your life
and evaluate the significance that they display
find the direction they point for you
and what they are trying to say.

Follow your bliss as it presents itself
use life's circumstance to grow
become what you are meant to be
surrender and you will know.

Grasp more meaning from your life
give credence to its pain
forge your future yet manifest
from the knowledge you have gained.

We cannot change what has transpired
but we can modify how we react
knowing that God has a greater purpose
that in us He did enact.

Tragedy will still rise up to meet us
tears will continue to flow from our eyes
but in distinguishing the pattern of synchronicity
you will begin to realize.

To comprehend the greater plan
a personal paradigm of our own
and implement what we have to do
with the seeds that should be sown.

Experience your sorrow as it comes
express the feelings of your grief
know that death is a part of life
that comes in like a thief.

Our bodies are very fragile
life is terminal from the start
and when you lose your loved one
you must know this in your heart.

You are sad, hurt and lonely
and you have a right to be
but you can choose to grow from this
and fulfill your destiny.

Afterword

At this point I assume that you have read the letters, poems, postscripts and prologue. The intent of this book upon the start was to publish the Kelly letters to help people through the process of their grief. There is no worse pain on this earth than to lose a child, no grief harder to bear. As I was working on all the material in this book, I soon realized there was more than just the letters that needed to be heard. The incredible experiences that we underwent in those last six months of Kelly's life, is a miraculous, unbelievable, and bittersweet tale to tell. Now I will attempt to enlighten you on the gifts that we were given to me from God that were attained only from the loss of *my* son (God is very empathetic on this point). You can see how Kelly's life and his consummate death touched our lives and the lives of others, in the great ripple affect.

I would guess the largest and most obvious obstacle to overcome was Kelly's death—that he just plainly was no longer here with us. It is so hard to accept the unacceptable, the loss of your child. It is in recognizing the spiritual gifts that you are given in the process of losing a loved one that gives you the strength to move on. You cannot change the fact of their death but you can modify how you react. There is no way to bring them back so you have to look at ways of keeping their legacy and memory alive. You give credence to their life by how you live yours. You can crawl in a hole of self-pity forever, keeping their memory alive in your own selfish way by your apathy and fear of moving on. This does nothing for their living memory; it simply just makes you a miserable person to be around and ultimately two lives are wasted. The feelings of deep despair will still continue for a long, long time and you may at times wish for your own death to gain relief. This is okay to feel and a perfectly normal reaction following a devastating loss. You recognize it for what it is, you let it in, feel it, and let it go.

Grief contains a variety of emotions that come as they may. There is no sure map to follow or chart that will reveal your individual path. Emotions surface when you least expect it. When it happens do not be embarrassed or cover them up, experience them; good friends understand and will give you a hug or give you your space. There is no one way to grieve; only your way. Grief is hard work and there is no way around it, only thorough it—and it takes as long as it takes.

There are greater things in store for you in this life, many things to accomplish and many lives to touch. You have to look at your situation as an opportunity for your own personal growth. By growing from the loss of their life, you in essence keep their legacy and their ability to affect others' lives alive. You substantiate their life by the way you live yours. This not only benefits others by your interaction with their life, but keeps the memory of your loved one alive and ever present in your heart.

I love my life more than ever before and Kelly is alive and with me every second of every day. My life and the life of my family had been changed forever in so many positive ways. Kelly's death has propelled me into a world of caring, compassion and love. I look at life as what can I do for others; how I can help to heal others pain and make the world a better place. When we were living in California, I went to massage school to be able to massage Kelly and ease some of his discomfort. Since that time I have provided massage for many terminally ill and grieving people. I joined the AIDS massage project (AMP) and have helped dozens of people with the pains of their disease and the process of their dying. I have facilitated grief groups and have helped others to cope with the loss of a loved one. I have paid special attention to parents whom have lost a child. I have helped them prepare for the passing over of their child, assisting with making the funeral plans and helping to rebuild their lives the months and, sometimes years, that follow.

Not only can you provide assistance for people in grief, despair and the pangs of death, but also it can help in every aspect of your life. For the past twelve years I have given blood on a monthly basis totaling over twenty-five gallons of blood donated. Being involved with the Red Cross, I have organized blood drives and, more recently, bone marrow testing drives to recruit more volunteers for the National Bone Marrow Donor database. I have been on the database for 15 years and have never been called for a potential match. My daughter Meagan was tested at one of the drives I coordinated and she was just recently found to be a match for a patient. At this writing she is in round two of testing and waiting for more test results. This is another way one can participate in a miracle and literally help save someone's life. This form of giving is so valuable as it saves or extends the life of hundreds each year with such a small personal sacrifice.

As you become more centered in your altruistic nature and begin giving to others, you will discover it becomes a lifestyle. You will find yourself opening more doors for people (physically and metaphorically), becoming a better driver, a better citizen, and ultimately a better person. This becomes addicting, for when you give you get so much back and life again becomes a joy. These are the gifts my son has given me. The best part of this process is that through your good works, you can affect change in other people—and them in others and so on and so on in a progressive ripple effect.

Energy does not dissipate; it only changes form and moves ever onward. Everyone has to face the fact they will ultimately lose someone they love some time in their life. We should not have to wait until we lose that person, to share our love with others in a positive way that can help heal people and the planet as a whole. Love God with all your heart; believe in miracles and the magic in life. Have faith that miracles can happen—it will change your life.

It is sufficiently clear that all things are changed, and nothing really perishes,
and that the sum of matter remains absolutely the same.
—Frances Bacon

Thirteen years later, I still marvel at all the happened to us through the experiences of our son. Several years ago, following a corporate merger, I lost my job of some twenty—odd years. When I left I was responsible for safety, a position I had held for three years and took very seriously. In that time the injury rates dropped dramatically, so much, in fact, we received a national award. Wherever you are at, with the right motive you can affect positive change or plant seeds of change.

Losing a job is a devastating reality. We had just recently purchased a five-acre hobby farm out in the country. We were supporting four horses, cats, dogs, and a whole litany of other animals and activities. My daughter was soon to graduate from high school and would be starting college in the near future. My wife works as a Registered Nurse in I.C.U. at a local hospital. She makes an adequate income, but I needed a job to literally save the farm. I put my faith in God and my gut feelings that are now an intrinsic part of my life.

There were a few rough months but I let go and let God. Soon I found myself working at St. Elizabeth Ann Seton School, a small K-8 parochial school not fifteen minutes from the farm. I had retained my boilers' license from my previous position and used it to land the job as the boiler engineer/maintenance man at this little school. I love it at the school. I see 400 kids every day and they are a continual joy to me. In my memories, my son will always physically be a nine-year-old boy. When I see all the boys at school and watch them grow through the years I can imagine my son growing with them. This is truly a gift.

I have become an active part of the children's' life in school. They recognize me as an artist, so in the early hours before school I put gold stars on all my favorite artwork in the hallways. The kids now anticipate getting a star on their artwork and are doing excellent work to get one. Being a Catholic school, the atmosphere is a very joy filled one and one with emphasis on spirit. There is singing all the time, which continually lifts the spirit and nourishes the soul. I also have become involved with the kids with their singing. I have taught K-8 students how to use sign language with several songs that they sing at mass. I intend to start a signing choir sometime in the future. The kids love me and I them. It is the best job I have ever had. I feel better physically, mentally, emotionally and am charged with the exhilaration of knowing I am on the right path. It is life changing and miraculous. Life is good.

Dear Mitch,

Thank you for being our custodian, friend, janitor, and artist. You really make our school fun. It's way more than pleasure to have you work at our school. I especially appreciate how you talk to us, encourage us, help us and listen to our ideas.

I don't know if you remember but I really enjoy the time that people were asking you to draw things for them, and you said "I will if you bring in a picture of it." Well, I think I was the only one to bring a picture. I brought one of my dog Cracker, and you drew it for me. My mom got a frame for it, so it is really, really cool. So I appreciate all the things

you've done for me not just that one.
In my point of veiw you make it easier for us to learn. You keep the school clean and fresh. Without you our school would never be the same. Thank you for everything you've done.

God Bless !!

Sarah Osberg

This letter was written by Sarah Osberg, one of the many wonderful letters that I recently received from the students in Mrs. Hunter's 5th grade class. These letters are the best work bonus I have ever been honored to receive.

With my job at the school, there is another fulfilling anecdote I need to share. In writing this manuscript, I gave it to family, friends and a few teachers at the school for feedback prior to publishing. One of those teachers, Sandi Anderson, has a warm and radiant spirit. She is wonderful with the kids and is an excellent educator. We became friends right away. After she had read the manuscript she asked me " Did you ever facilitate a cancer stress therapy group at a local hospital ten years ago?" I replied that I had facilitated several groups around that time. Gasping she said, "Oh my ...then it is you!" Sandi went on to say that she had accompanied a friend as a support person to one of my sessions. At that session, she vividly remembers the story I told of the miracle of the cornstalks and what we had done in Mexico. She further explained that she has been telling that miraculous story to every one of her classes over these past ten years. We can sometimes make a difference in people's life whether we realize it or not.

Change is the only constant we have in life. In adapting to that change and using it as an opportunity for growth and benevolence you will begin to see the pattern that was meant for your life. As opposed to the twelve to fourteen hour days that I had spent at the refinery, at the school, I now work a standard eight-hour day. The pay is a whole lot less but you adjust your lifestyle accordingly. I lost some income, but have gained so much more; the adage: *less is more* has now become very real. This change has afforded me the time to work on my gardens, ride my horse, see more sunsets on my deck, visit with friends, pursue my altruistic endeavors, work on my artwork and, of course, finish my book. I had made a promise to myself and to my son that I would write our story, publish it and share it with the world. This I have done. If it has helped you please share it with others as we travel this road together.

—Mitchell D. Carmody, 2001

Sing as if no one were listening, dance as if no one were watching,
And live everyday as if it were your last.
—Old Irish Proverb

WHERE DO WE GO FROM HERE?

Where has all the magic gone
that once had filled my life?
Sacred days…so bittersweet
with my son, my daughter and my wife.

We fought death with all we had
there was almost nothing we did not try
but despite our every effort
our child still had to die.

We were left in pain and sorrow
but we sought magic through our tears
and found miracles in motion
as we moved on throughout the years.

Those miracles in motion
kept our boat afloat
no dream seemed too bizarre
or a coincidence too remote.

Spontaneous chills and goose bumps
are meant to warm the spirit
they happen when they happen
and happen when you need it.

Years pass and newfound goals
have seemed to slowly fill the space
where once were his deep blue eyes
and the touch of his embrace.

Those days seem so long ago
and so much water has passed under
but alas, I shall not forget
all the magic and the wonder.

When God is breathing down your neck
It's because He is holding you real close
You can feel His heartbeat within you own
and find ways that you can cope.

You find a way to transform your grief
into something tangible and good
so light a bon-fire in the darkness
let your deeds become the wood.

You must give back to everyone
with everything you can
share your world with others
truly *listen*, and lend a hand.

You cannot bring a loved one back
there are no rebates from the grave
so one must embrace a living face
and find someone you can save.

Save somebody from their loneliness
save someone from their pain
save them from themselves
or from a society gone insane.

Everyone longs for love
without it we would surely die
it's easy to give in many ways
a smile, a hug… a cry.

So it's "Top-o-the morning" to everyone
let your heart-light shine
reach into each other's hearts
with words, with touch…and time.

Make silly jokes and laugh out loud
it's giggles that massage the soul
look directly into peoples' eyes
and let your heart-light glow.

Others will see that Inner Light
as you gaze into their eyes
and know we are all relations
the ignorant and the wise.

These words are ruminations
that originates from my heart
and I try to live them daily
for the benefits they impart.

Still there will be difficult times
when sadness escorts travail
nothing tried will ease the pain
and you will feel that you have failed.

This has happened to me
and not that long ago
I wondered where the magic went
and why it had to go.

Where were the miracles that
were once woven within my grief
I used to talk to angels
and had visions in my sleep.

I know that the well never goes dry
God's touch is always there
it's I who have dried my tears
and moved on from my despair.

I can manage by myself, I've said…
others need you by their side
but dear God I miss the magic
that in my life you allowed to reside.

I now realize the miracles never stop
they only take a different form
mini-miracles happen everyday
and soon becomes the norm.

God's magic has changed my life
changed who and what I am
I have moved through the pain
and find joy in all I can.

Sunrises are crisp again
sunsets bathe my heart
butterflies, birds, and song
are daily works of art.

As the sands of the ocean
was once a piece of land
what once *was* in human terms
can never be again.

Some flowers bloom for only moments
then wither and fade away
but the memory of their great beauty
is always here to stay.

So we move on with our life
and embrace the miracles that we can find
the magic in essence, never goes away
it's just that sometimes we are blind.

Blind to what is right beside us
or hitting us smack dab in the face
there is no shame in heartfelt empathy
for love it knows no disgrace.

There will be people that we meet
that we have known for many years
or share moments for the first time
with strangers and their fears.

We must boldly share our love,
reach out to others without hesitation or dismay
find the pain that lies so near
and around us everyday.

Whether it's an old friend or an enemy,
a relative or just a cashier at the store
there will be some one that will need you
and it's *you* who shall open the door.

Be of service to yourself
and all with all the people that you meet
there are many paths yet to cross
many avenues and streets.

There are people who desperately need
your evolvement in their sorrow
just as you need them
to face the next tomorrow.

So if you think that God has overlooked you
and has no idea that you are here
you must realize it's not that He's forgotten
it's you who have forgotten that He's so near.

Miracles and magic are never ever gone
they are always within our reach
just as are the memories of our loved ones
and what they had to teach.

They taught us love is unconditional
it is the strongest fiber in our being
so let loose, let go, let God, let love
let YOURSELF …and start a new beginning.

When one door closes another opens somewhere…be there.

Great grief is a divine and terrible radiance
which transfigures the wretched.

—Victor Hugo

PRAYER FOR HEALERS

Lord make me an instrument of your peace:
where there is hatred, let me sow love;
where there is injury, healing;
where there is doubt, faith;
where there is despair, hope;
where there is darkness, light;
and where there is sadness, joy.

Oh divine Master,
grant that I may not seek
so much to be consoled
as to console;
to be understood as to understand;
to be loved as to love.

For it is in giving that we receive;
it is in healing that we are healed;
and it is in dying
that we are born to eternal life.

—St. Frances of Assisi

Postscript
December 1st, 2001

On December 1, 1987, my world was shattered by the death of my son. I had lost my father at age 15; being the youngest of seven children, I knew him as a father, but never as a friend. My son then dies at age nine and I again lose a longed for future friend. I will never know Kelly as an *adult* friend, although I think that through the process of Kelly's illness and with the knowledge of his impending death we did in a way become friends, for we were buddies. Despite all the pain and horror in the last two years of his life, we truly lived life to the fullest; we shared more life in a short time than many families would in a lifetime. I recognize that now and it gives me some solace from the painful memories.

Today is December 1, 2001, fourteen years to the day, following Kelly's death. I have finished the final touches on the manuscript and will meet with the publishers on Tuesday. Toward the end of the book you may have read the poem, "Where do we go from here?" In that sonnet, I ask the question, "Where has all the magic gone that once had filled my life?" So many miraculous experiences surrounded us at the time that we tended to take them for granted. Life moves on regardless of situation, and so do we.

In the poem, I lament that I have not experienced any more mystical communications or experiences from Kelly. Had Kelly moved on or had I? I was content with the message of the cornstalks and I truly expected nothing more. That's part of the letting go. Finishing the book that I had promised Kelly I would write is a huge step in final closure for both of us.

When Kelly was first diagnosed a neighbor and good friend of ours in Bayport gave Kelly a beautiful blue-eyed white Siamese cat that she had picked up at the shelter. Kelly named him *Ernie* and they became fast friends and inseparable. When they were sitting together in the right light, their intense blue eyes of the same shade glowed brightly. It was very striking. After Kelly's death, Ernie became a loner and a recluse, hiding in the shadows and very rarely interacting with anyone.

A few months ago, Ernie now almost 19 years old, became sick and we had to put him down. When my wife returned home from the vet with Ernie in a box, I dug a hole in our back pasture in preparation for burial. Ernie, still warm, was lying as if as if just asleep in a box in our basement when Kathy, an old friend stopped by unannounced. She was that good friend from the Bayport days who had given Ernie to Kelly some fourteen years earlier. She was surprised and saddened by the death of Ernie. She said, "Guys, I had no idea about Ernie but look what I have in the truck." We went to her vehicle and found sitting on the front seat a beautiful five-week old Siberian Husky. She had the same white coloring of Ernie and more strikingly had the same intense blue eyes. She said, "Someone had dropped her off on a country road and I was taking her to the shelter, but I thought you guys would have the room out here. And she is so beautiful." I took one look at those dog's eyes and told our friend Kathy, "We'll take her!"

I am a real softy when it comes to animals and have always had a dog at the foot of our bed. Louise as we call her now, regularly sleeps in our bed at night. Oddly, she always moves up right next to my head, by my pillow, in the same spot that Ernie had always slept. She is still a puppy so at this time does not take up too much room. She is well behaved, I enjoy her presence and allow her to sleep there.

Last night I had a dream that I was in a bookstore and a woman was looking at my book and said, "My God, what an incredible story you two have to tell!" I then realized that my son Kelly, now my height, was standing right next to me, shoulder to shoulder. I had my left arm crooked around his neck, our heads were turned looking right into each other's eyes and he smiled and said rather sheepishly, "I was pretty young. I don't remember that much of it anymore." I was so shocked at seeing him, I could say nothing and with my arm still around his neck I pulled him closer. Looking into his eyes, I felt his energy and smelled his familiar scent. It was then that I woke up and found myself looking straight into the big blue eyes of my dog Louise. Her head was tightly crooked into my arm; her nose was on my chest. With her tail wagging wildly she smothered me with sloppy puppy kisses. No, the magic is never ever gone, and, once again for Kelly and me, it was "hello and not goodbye."

—Mitchell D. Carmody

Feel free to write to me at *heartlightstudio@aol.com* with questions, comments or support in your time of need.

We walk this road together.

Do or do not—
there is no "try."
————Yoda

About the Author

The author has personally experienced a lot of death in his family at an early age and ongoing. During that time he has studied much about the processes of death, dying, loss and bereavement. In the process he has found himself on a spiritual road of discovery that has continued to bless his life and ours. Mitch is a trained hospice volunteer, a trained massage therapist and Aids Massage volunteer. He has facilitated many grief, cancer, massage and stress relief groups and has taught classes at community education in these areas. Personally assisting people and their families struggling with terminal illness and grief is an important part of his ministry. Assisting to help plan and participate in many funerals he considers an honor and tries to help in making the experience a celebration of life. He is a staunch supporter and volunteer with the American Red Cross as well as donating blood monthly. Helping others is paramount in his life and he tries to help heal the human condition wherever he finds it.

The author is also a gifted photographer and an accomplished artist. He is responsible for the book's cover photograph of his son Kelly as well as many other award winning photographs. He has completed well over one hundred portraits of people, using a variety of mediums. More recently Mitch has concentrated his artistic endeavors using his favorite medium; *pencil drawing.* All the illustrations used in this book are recent examples of the artist's work. The photo-realism style you find in these portraits is evident in all of his work. He works out of his studio in Denmark Township where limited edition prints are available as well as custom portraits.

Mitch's wife Barb, is an I.C.U. (Intensive Care Unit) registered nurse working at Lakeview Hospital in Stillwater

Minnesota. They were high school sweethearts and have been married for twenty-six years. His daughter Meagan, also a writer, is in her 1st year of nursing school. Together they live on a small hobby farm in rural Denmark Township, just east of the Twin Cities. The greatest love in their life besides their family and wonderful friends is their horses, their dogs, and their gardens. Letting go of their pain—they have embraced life.

*Man is here for the sake of other men—above all for those upon whose smile
and well being our own happiness depends, and also for the countless unknown
souls, with whose fate we are connected by a bond of sympathy.*
—Albert Einstein

Call For Letters

I have recently begun work on my second book that is titled: *Letters from the Heart.*

This book will be a collection of letters from *you* the reader. I am asking that you send in your stories of survival. If you have survived a devastating loss in your life and have found once again a meaningful existence; please send me your story. If you have survived a terminal illness or had a close brush with death; please send me your story. If you have received some form of communication from a lost loved one; please send me your story. If you have a story of someone and or something that has been a *parachute* in your life and provided a pathway for your healing please send me your story. I know that there are many more life-changing testimonies of survival that need to be shared.

Please send all correspondence to:

Heart Light Studios Inc.
14765 70th St. South
Hastings, Minnesota 55033
Email: *heartlightstudio@aol.com*
Phone number: 651-436-3658